THIS IS
DINOSAUR

THIS IS DINOSAUR

ECHO PARK COUNTRY
AND ITS MAGIC RIVERS

EDITED BY WALLACE STEGNER
FOREWORDS BY WALLACE STEGNER
AND TERRY TEMPEST WILLIAMS

LYONS
PRESS

Guilford, Connecticut

An imprint of The Rowman & Littlefield Publishing Group, Inc.
4501 Forbes Blvd., Ste. 200
Lanham, MD 20706
www.rowman.com

Distributed by NATIONAL BOOK NETWORK

First Lyons Press edition 2019. Published by arrangement with Alfred A. Knopf, an imprint of The Knopf Doubleday Publishing Group, a division of Penguin Random House LLC.

All photographs are courtesy of the National Park Service unless otherwise credited.

British Library Cataloguing in Publication Information Available

Library of Congress Cataloging-in-Publication Data

Names: Stegner, Wallace, 1909–1993, editor.
Title: This is dinosaur : Echo Park country and its magic rivers / edited by
   Wallace Stegner ; forewords by Wallace Stegner and Terry Tempest Williams.
Description: Guilford, Connecticut : Lyons Press, 2019. | Originally
   published by Alfred A. Knopf, Inc., 1955.
Identifiers: LCCN 2018050100 | ISBN 9781493039494 (paperback)
Subjects: LCSH: Dinosaur National Monument (Colo. and Utah)
Classification: LCC F832.D5 T45 2019 | DDC 978.8/12—dc23 LC record available
   at https://lccn.loc.gov/2018050100

Contents

Foreword by Terry Tempest Williams   vii

Foreword by Wallace Stegner   xi

The Marks of Human Passage   1
Wallace Stegner

Geological Exhibit   17
Eliot Blackwelder

The Natural World of Dinosaur   33
Olaus Murie and Joseph W. Penfold

The Ancients of the Canyons   53
Robert H. Lister

Fast Water   65
Otis "Dock" Marston

A Short Look at Eden   81
David Bradley

The National Park Idea   99
Alfred A. Knopf

Foreword

By Terry Tempest Williams

TUCKED INSIDE my copy of *This Is Dinosaur*, the hardback first edition published in 1955, is a pamphlet that reads, "What Is Your Stake in Dinosaur?" As it unfolds, you see that it is not a pamphlet at all, but a map with inspirational words, photographs, and vital statistics. It is also a call to action outlining what you can do.

Vivid paragraphs accompany black-and-white photographs of Echo Park and the rivers that define this place, the Yampa and the Green. "A Land of Surprises. . . ." it reads, "where it's hard to tell how the river will turn next. Matchless scenery, ever unfolding—sylvan corridors, enticing side canyons, colorful cliffs, wildlife at home—all these are easily, safely, quietly reachable now. The proposed 300–500 feet of fluctuating water would erase these scenes."

As you fold the pamphlet back together and turn it over, you see in large type, "Help Prevent a Misplaced Dam in Dinosaur." Below it reads, "America's conservation forces are sincerely interested in wise development of the water resources of the states of the Upper Colorado River Basin; they know that wise development will not impair our enviable, irreplaceable national park and wilderness system."

You then see the purpose of these beautiful artifacts of advocacy: "A Beautiful Book about a Beautiful Park. To appreciate fully the grandeur of one of our finest national parks, we urge you and your friends to read *This Is Dinosaur* edited by Wallace Stegner." The price: $5.00.

The Colorado River Storage Project proposed by the Army Corp of Engineers is the center of these conservationists' concern, among them the writer Wallace Stegner, the publisher Alfred A. Knopf, the biologist Olaus J. Murie, the geologist Eliot Blackwelder, the anthropologist Robert Lister, and boatmen extraordinaire Martin Litton and "Dock" Marston. Photographers punctuate the writing, Philip Hyde, Don Hatch, among them, including Charles Eggert, who made a film named after the book itself, *This Is Dinosaur*, as a visual companion piece produced for the National Parks Association.

Wallace Stegner was a mentor of mine. We served together on the Governing Council of the Wilderness Society and the board of the Southern Utah Wilderness Alliance. He also played tennis with my grandfather "Sanky" Dixon in Salt Lake City, Utah.

Wally believed that a writer had responsibilities beyond the construction of beautiful sentences on the page. He believed writers also had a responsibility as citizens to speak out on issues of justice. Stopping the dam at Echo Park that would compromise Dinosaur National Monument established in 1915 was among his rights and responsibilities as an American whose debt to western landscapes was large and figured prominently in his fiction and essays.

I agree with him.

In 1995, the writer Stephen Trimble and I took inspiration from this template of advocacy. When Utah's wilderness was under siege by a hostile bill before Congress, we sought the help of fellow writers to help bring national attention to the plight of southern Utah's red rock desert. With brilliant words by such writers as Mardy Murie, N. Scott Momaday, Barry Lopez, and Rick Bass, this tiny volume of stories we called *Testimony* found its way into the Congressional Record as Senator Bill Bradley from the state of New Jersey read each piece (including an essay from John McPhee, one of his own constituents) during a filibuster on the Senate floor. The bad bill was defeated. And when Grand Staircase-Escalante National Monument was established by President Bill Clinton on September 26, 1996, the president held up *Testimony* and said, "This book made a difference."

This Is Dinosaur continues to instruct and inspire another generation, including the words that end Wallace Stegner's beginning essay, "The

[handwritten margin note: She is saying should go beyond]

Marks of Human Passage." They are as relevant now in the twenty century as when they were written over six decades ago:

> We are the most dangerous species of life on the planet, and every other species, even the earth itself, has cause to fear our power to exterminate. We are also the only species which when it chooses to do, will go to great effort to save what it might destroy.

This Is Dinosaur is a book of extraordinary effort that yielded extraordinary results.

The dams at Echo Park and Split Mountain were never built. The modern environmental era was set in motion. Activism is patriotism. Passionate engagement by citizens matters. The integrity of Dinosaur National Monument remains intact and the Green and Yampa Rivers flow freely as they did in 1955.

But threats remain. Serious threats. Dinosaur National Monument is surrounded by one of the most intensive natural gas and oil developments in the Interior West. An over flight of this area reveals an oil and gas infrastructure that appears like an exposed nervous system. A few miles south as the raven flies, America's first tar sands mine is under construction in the magnificent Book Cliffs.

Questions must be asked if we are to maintain "the open space of democracy" and protect what our species is in the process of destroying: What effect does fracking have on the aquifer and water quality for the local community? How does oil and gas development impact air quality and human health? What responsibility do we have to the future given fossil fuel development's increased carbon emissions released into the atmosphere that contributes to a warming planet?

If Wallace Stegner was alive in this moment, he would be asking these questions alongside his fellow contributors to *This Is Dinosaur*. This elegant book opens a door to what an engaged and informed community looks like, a way we might move forward with grace and integrity, drawing from both the facts of science and the imagination of the arts and humanities.

One word comes to mind: Love. May we love these lands and protect them, for their sake and our own. It is not only about our future, but the dignity of the broader community, both human and wild. We are not the only species that lives and breathes and dreams on this beautiful, broken planet we call home.

This Is Dinosaur is a powerful testament of a community who cared and in so doing, not only made a difference, but created "a geography of hope" on the page and a model of engagement in the world.

Not long ago, I visited Dinosaur National Monument. The Green River was low; cobbles once covered were now exposed. Scientists no longer are using the word "drought" in the American Southwest. We are now living in a state of "aridification." I picked up one of the round dry stones and wrapped it with red thread. Bloodlines.

May we never forget the power of these wildlands in the American West. May we never take their beauty for granted. And may we as citizens of these United States continue to acknowledge the spiritual force they possess as they remind us through the generations what it means to be human.

Terry Tempest Williams
Castle Valley, Utah
November 1, 2018

Foreword

By Wallace Stegner

THIS IS DINOSAUR was originally published in 1955, in the midst of a bitter controversy. David Brower and the Sierra Club originated the idea. Lovers of the national parks contributed their skill and knowledge as text and pictures. I edited their contributions. Alfred Knopf published the result in an astonishingly short time and with small regard to profit.

Our motives were both short-term and long-term. On the one hand, we wanted to save Dinosaur National Monument from the two dams then planned within its boundaries by the Bureau of Reclamation as parts of the Upper Colorado River Storage Project—dams which would have flooded and destroyed irreplaceable scenic, biological, and archaeological resources. On the other hand, we wanted to set in brass the principle that any part of the national park system should be immune from any sort of intrusion and damage, public or private.

In my original foreword I denied that this was a "fighting" book. We only wanted to describe the treasures of natural beauty, history, archaeology, and peace of mind that lay in Dinosaur, and what the Echo Park and Split Mountain dams would destroy. But we were by no means without ulterior motives—our non-fighting stance was tactical, not strategic. We believed that if the public and the Congress knew what Dinosaur contained, the Congress, under public pressure, would remove the threat to it. So we named no enemies. We only tried to describe; and every member of Congress got a copy of our book.

As it turned out, we were right. Fighting book or not, *This Is Dinosaur* was an effective weapon in the first great conservation battle of recent times, the battle that consolidated several weak and diverse organizations, with their "hinterland" of interested but non-activist public, into a movement with astonishing political muscle. That movement rose up and stopped the Upper Colorado River Storage Project cold. It kept the dams out of Dinosaur, and if it had known its own strength might have kept the Glen Canyon Dam out of Glen Canyon, down the Colorado, as well. Its political strength left the Green and Yampa flowing free, left untouched the green bottoms and the colored cliffs, preserved the archaeological sites of the Fremont people, left undamaged the spawning grounds of the Colorado River Squawfish and the Humpbacked Chub. Thanks to the Sierra Club, Wilderness Society, Izaak Walton League, and other organizations and individuals, and in some small part to this book, Dinosaur National Monument is still the remote and lovely sanctuary that it was in 1955.

The barricade on which the conservation groups lined up was the National Park Act of 1916, which stated that the purpose of the national parks was "to conserve the scenery and the natural and historic objects and the wildlife therein and to provide for the enjoyment of the same in such manner and by such means as will leave them unimpaired for the enjoyment of future generations." We wanted no precedents that would justify any sort of impairment, and we believed that there should be the same protection for national monuments, historical sites, and other elements of the system as for the national parks.

The fight that saved Dinosaur strengthened the hand of the National Park Service against the Federal Power Commission, the Bureau of Reclamation, the Corps of Engineers, and other powerful agencies eager to "develop" the water and power within the national parks. It put a damper on the ambitions of miners, loggers, graziers, and other private interests that wanted to exploit the parks for their own profit. If the Dinosaur battle had been lost in 1954–55, there would have been extreme pressure on Glacier, Yellowstone, Olympic, and other parks; and we might never have seen the General Authorities Act of 1970, which declared that all the varieties of reservation making up the National Park System are equally parts of that system, and protected by the same umbrella of law.

So is this a success story, a fable of dragons slain and dangers put down? Not quite. In 1955 Dinosaur was a remote and half-forgotten national monument in danger from federal dams. Thirty years later it is still remote, still half-forgotten, and still in danger from federal dams. But there is one difference. In 1955 the monument was in danger from dams within its boundaries. In 1985 it is in danger from dams outside. The 1955 danger was too much water; the 1985 danger is too little water, or water in regulated and unnatural amounts.

If there is one lesson that we have learned from the events of the past thirty years it is that not even a national park can maintain itself as an island. In 1980 a report entitled *The State of the Parks* listed dozens of threats to the integrity of the parks and other elements of the system, and most of them were threats from beyond the park boundaries, effects that migrated from unprotected land to the protected parks as hillside mud migrates to obliterate a meadow.

Thus Yellowstone is under threat from proposals to tap geothermal sources of power outside the park, with absolutely unpredictable effects on the geysers and hot springs of the park itself.

Thus Redwood and other parks are under threat from the erosion of steep clear-cut terrain beyond the park limits. Thus the water table of the Southwestern parks—the water table on which most life in that region depends—falls as groundwater is pumped, miles away, for slurry lines and mines and power plants. Thus the air of Canyonlands, Arches, Capitol Reef, Bryce, and Grand Canyon is polluted by power plants at Page and Four Corners. Any tourist can now watch rangers at Capitol Reef monitoring air pollution that they are totally helpless to do anything about. Thus the Colorado River in Marble and Grand Canyons, and the recreational boating dependent on its flow, are both at the mercy of the power engineers of Glen Canyon Dam and the peaking-power needs of Los Angeles and Las Vegas.

And Dinosaur, off the track, half-forgotten, is now threatened from above, by the Juniper and Cross Mountain dams proposed for the Yampa west of Craig, Colorado. The excuse is that water not "saved" is "lost." The fallacy of that argument is that the life of any dam, or of irrigated land in the arid regions, is but a tick in eternity. Dams silt up, irrigated fields get salty and sterile. A civilization built on them is built on something frailer than sand, and the over-population they encourage can only end in another variety of ghost towns.

But in the process of building up to a 21st century letdown, the Juniper and Cross Mountain dams would destroy or degrade the Yampa's riparian habitat and all its resident creatures. They would change the flow of the Yampa and hence of the Green, alter the bed load and turbidity, threaten or destroy the spawning beds of at least three endangered species of fish found only in these rivers, and kill the wild rivers which provide one of the most exhilarating and healthful sports of outdoor Americans.

Those effects, predictable but unmeasurable in advance, would constitute impairment of the most serious kind. If the National Park Service had control, they would never happen; but the effects come from far off, invading the island of protection. Again the National Park Act is the barricade upon which conservationists and environmentalists must gather to resist the dangers. And despite their success in 1955, despite the reassurances of the General Authorities Act, they know it is easier to defend a national park than a national monument. The national parks are the crown jewels.

A national park, which must be established by Congress, is an expression of the public will in a way that a national monument, established by Presidential decree, is not. In the hierarchy of excellence, a national park has the highest status. Strangers will come farther to visit it; local people take more pride in it—and reap more profit from it. It is what foreign visitors come seeking—the best we have, the most scrupulously protected.

Dinosaur should be a national park. The congressional delegations of Utah and Colorado should be collaborating to start the machinery in motion. Environmental and outdoor organizations should be mounting a campaign, the businessmen and ordinary citizens of Vernal, the nearest supply base, should be projecting the economic effects of a change of status, as well as those of a killing-by-upstream-dams. This is a case where economic interest and aesthetic and spiritual and recreational interest coincide. Dinosaur is not only more saveable as a national park than as a national monument; it is a better and more durable basis for the economic health of the region.

Even as a national park, Dinosaur may not be safe, but it will be safer. It will be able to mobilize friends, its defenders will have more confidence, its potential exploiters will have to move more cautiously. Pride can gather around a national park. Tourists from Tokyo and Frankfort can float down the canyons of the Yampa and Green rivers and know America better and with greater enthusiasm. There is no such place as this outside the American Southwest, and this is one of the superlative places even in that region of wonders.

In the widespread program of acquisition and upgrading of park lands that took place in the 1960s and 1970s, Dinosaur got overlooked. Yet it is fully, superbly worthy to be a national park. It is full of potential for human refreshment and recreation, it is an outdoor museum of an extraordinary kind, it imposes the dignity and patience of the ages on our petty, sweaty human preoccupations. It is country that generates reverence and love, and two rivers run through it to give it life. It cannot be left just as it is, but it should be protected and sheltered into being as close to natural as our intrusions and our very love will permit.

— Wallace Stegner, 1985

THIS IS DINOSAUR

The Marks
of Human Passage

Wallace Stegner

DINOSAUR NATIONAL MONUMENT is one of the last almost
"unspoiled" wildernesses—which means it is relatively unmarked by man.
Yet it is already, despite being one of the latest-explored parts of the continent, a palimpsest of human history, speculation, rumor, fantasy, ambi-
tion, science, controversy, and conflicting plans for use, and these human
records so condition our responses to the place that they contain a good
part of Dinosaur's meaning.

What shall we say of it? That it is a three-pronged district of about
200,000 acres, straddling the Utah-Colorado border a little south of where
that border meets the southern boundary of Wyoming. That it is a part—
one of the junior partners—of the National Park System begun with the
reservation of Yellowstone in 1872 and confirmed by the establishment of
the National Park Service in 1916. That topographically it is defined by the
deep canyons of two rivers, the Green and the Yampa, which meet secretly
in the sunny, sunken pocket of Echo Park and then together cut Whirlpool
Canyon, Island Park, Rainbow Park, and Split Mountain Canyon, from
whose mouth the water breaks out into the open Uinta Valley of Utah.
That the plateau through which the canyons are cut is an eastward extension of the Uinta Mountains, one of the few east-west-trending ranges in
the United States. That the larger of the two rivers, the Green, is the longest
fork of the Colorado; and that it used to be called the Seedskeedee-Agie,

the Prairie Hen River, by the Crows, and by the Spaniards the Rio Verde. Its tributary the Yampa is even yet by some people and some maps called the Bear.

One can observe that Echo Park, at the heart of this reserve, lies at approximately 109° West Longitude and 40°31' North Latitude; that the altitude ranges from 4,700 feet at the mouth of Split Mountain Canyon to 9,600 feet at the tip of Zenobia Peak near the northeastern boundary; that the rocks exposed run in age from the Uinta Mountain quartzite of the Pre-Cambrian period to the Brown's Park sandstone of the Pliocene; that the life zones represented spread from the Sonoran in the canyon bottoms to sub-arctic on the higher ridges. The colors of the rocks vary from a rich red-brown to vermilion, from gray to almost sugar-white, with many shades of pink and buff and salmon in between. The cliffs and sculptured forms are sometimes smooth, sometimes fantastically craggy, always massive, and they have a peculiar capacity to excite the imagination; the effect on the human spirit is neither numbing nor awesome, but warm and infinitely peaceful.

Having assembled these facts, both objective and subjective, we have said very little. Even the dry facts are simply the generalizations of human observation, distillations of topographical, cartographical, geological, biological, and other work that men have done in the region. Describing a place, we inevitably describe the marks human beings have put upon a place, the uses they have put it to, the things they have been taught by it. Even the dinosaurs whose bodies grounded on the bar of a Jurassic river here 120,000,000 years ago, and whose petrified bones gave the Monument its first reason for reservation as well as its permanent and rather misleading name, were only rocks until human curiosity unearthed and studied and compared and interpreted them.

To describe Dinosaur one must begin by summarizing its human history, and human history in Dinosaur is quaintly begun in the completely human impulse to immortalize oneself by painting or pecking or carving one's private mark, the symbol of one's incorrigible identity, on rocks and trees.

THE PREHISTORIC PEOPLE who inhabited the Green and Yampa canyons, and who belonged to the cultural complex known to archæologists as the Fremont Culture, a laggard branch of the prehistoric Pueblo-

Basketmaker group, or Anasazi, are properly the subject of another chapter (IV) of this book. We may borrow them here only long enough to note that the pictographs and petroglyphs which they painted in red ocher or chipped with sharp stones in the faces of the cliffs mark the northernmost extension of the Anasazi Culture, and that these murals, together with the terrace camp sites and middens and the many storage granaries in caves, are among the earliest human marks in the area. To us, the most immediately fascinating of the relics the Fremont people left are these pictures, which record the game they hunted, the ceremonial objects they revered, the idle doodling dreams they indulged in, and—most wistful and most human of all—the painted handprints and footprints, the personal tracks, that said, and still say: "I am." *[handwritten: → white people mark presence]*

These are all of Dinosaur's history for a long time; they reflect the period from about A.D. 400–800. Some archæologists believe that on the Uinta and Yampa plateaus there may be evidences of the passage southward, sometime about the year 1000, of the Athapascan hunters who were the ancestors of the modern Navajo and Apache, but the origin of those camp sites is still speculative. Leaving out that possibility, there passed nearly a thousand years after the last of the Fremont people departed during which, as far as history knows, these canyons were only wind and water and stone, space and sky and the slow sandpapering of erosion, the unheard scurry of lizard and scream of mountain lion, the unseen stiff-legged caution of deer, the unnoted roar of rapids in the dark slot of Lodore and the unrecorded blaze of canyon color darkening with rain and whitening with snow and glaring in the high sun of solstice. *[handwritten margin: what are the marks left by white/indigenous settlers]*

When the next man left a mark, he was a Spaniard, one of a watchful vanguard. The year was 1776. And nobody later reported seeing the mark he left; we know he left it only because Fray Silvestre Vélez de Escalante made an entry in his diary for September 14 as he was camped on the bank of the Green on his way to seek a route from New Mexico to Monterey in California.

"In this place," the explorer wrote (it was the day when the British were moving in to occupy New York, and General George Washington was preparing his retreat to Harlem Heights), "there are six large black cottonwood trees that have grown in pairs, attached to one another, and they are the ones closest to the river. Near them is another, standing alone, on

[handwritten bottom: – no land acknowledgment @ this time]

whose trunk, on the side facing the northwest, Don Joaquin Lain with an adz cleared a small space in the form of a rectangular window, and with a chisel carved on it the letters and numbers of this inscription, *The Year 1776*; and lower down in different letters the name *Lain*, with two crosses outside, the larger one above the inscription and the smaller one below it."

There are still cottonwoods answering that description near the southern boundary of the Monument, a half-mile or so below the dinosaur quarry and Monument Headquarters. Almost certainly they are not the same ones, for cottonwoods are not long-lived trees; but if they are, as some people believe, they have proved a less durable or less inert base for immortality than the cliffs the Fremont people scribbled on: the living wood has overgrown and obliterated any inscription. Fortunately the passage westward of those first Spaniards, the discoverers of the Green River among much else, was also recorded in Escalante's diary, in the Word, the most durable of all materials. The Word thus bounds Dinosaur not only on its southern geographical border but at the threshold of its entrance into recorded history.

These Spaniards probably did no more than poke their noses into the canyons, though Escalante reported in his diary "two high cliffs which, after forming a sort of corral, come so close together that one can scarcely see the opening through which the river comes"; and Miera set down on his map a mountain he called Sierra Mineral that was split straight through by the river. Both journal entry and the Sierra Mineral are surely references to Split Mountain.

Except for that tempting glimpse, Escalante skirted the southern edge of the cut-up Uinta and Yampa uplifts. Other travelers would skirt them along the north, leaving a no-man's-land between the known routes called the California Trail and the Spanish Trail. The canyons were a barrier, not a highway. But the next mark that men made in them recorded an attempt to use the river as highway, and to link the Spanish-dominated country southward with the routes of trappers and mountain men just finding their way across the continental divide among the headwaters of the Green.

That next mark came forty-nine years after Escalante. Like Lain's inscription on the tree (and, for all we know, like the murals of the Fremont people), it recorded a name and a date.

"Ashley, 1825," it says. It is painted on a rock in Red Canyon, above Brown's Park and outside the present Dinosaur National Monument. It commemorated the first known penetration of the Green River's canyons by white men—the bullboat expedition of General William Henry Ashley and six mountain men from about the site of present Fontanelle, Wyoming, to somewhere in Desolation Canyon, below the Uinta Valley. The purpose, like Escalante's, was practical: the exploration of a route, this time for profitable fur trade and a more southerly rendezvous among the Utes. Like Escalante's, the route turned out to have serious defects, and was not soon used again. Moreover, the written accounts of the journey waited a long time to be made public. Nevertheless, history lost and then found again is still history.

Ashley had divided his party of mountain men into four brigades because Crows had run off many of his horses and left him overloaded. With six men and the bulk of the supplies, he pushed off from a point about fifteen miles above the mouth of the Sandy, hoping to open up the southern country to the fur trade. Into the teeth of the unknown—into the teeth, in fact, of wild and fearful rumors, such as the one promoted by his own employee and partisan James Beckwourth of an awesome "suck" "where the river enters the Utah Mountains"—Ashley ran his laden bullboats. At Henry's Fork, where he appointed a rendezvous, and in Brown's Hole, where he found that several thousand Indians had wintered, he was in known country, or semi-known. But the run through Red Canyon's rapids had given them a good shaking and had made them unload and portage all their goods and lower the bullboats over one drop on rawhide cords. That was at Ashley Falls, named later by another explorer who had no idea who Ashley was; and that was where he took five minutes to paint his name on the rock.

The rest of his trip left no marks on the country. Through Lodore, which impressed them all with its gloom and scared them with its wild water, they went as unnoted as bubbles of foam; caught their breath in the lovely bottoms of Echo Park; ran or portaged through Whirlpool and Split Mountain canyons, still, of course, unnamed. In Split Mountain, Ashley was within an eyelash of drowning; his man Beckwourth later made claims to a heroic rescue. Actually when Ashley was running the canyons Beckwourth was clear over on the other side of the mountain with James Clyman's and then with Thomas Fitzpatrick's brigade.

Ashley's journal was not found and published until 1918. His scoot down the canyons in a flimsy pole framework covered with buffalo hide and calked with pitch was a casual episode in a career notable for fortitude and daring, and it had no effect on history because history never heard of it until much other history had overtaken and passed it. As it happened, the painted name and date on the rock by Ashley Falls stood there under rain and sun another twenty-four years before white men again came that way, and when they came they barely noticed the name and had no notion who had left it there.

They came on their way to somewhere else, part of the stream pouring across the northern passes bound for the gold fields of California in 1849. Their motive in running the river was not exploration, but impatience; their resource was not the cool daring of Ashley, but foolhardiness; and they knew nothing, neither geography nor history, to help or to deter them.

They were bullwhackers on a Forty-niner wagon train, fed up with dust and the poky plod of oxen, and displeased by the trainleader's decision to winter in Salt Lake City because of the lateness of the season. They said: By golly, if only a river would show up, and if they had a boat, and if it looked as if the water might flow to the Pacific, for a two-bit shinplaster they would. . . . So the river showed up, and rumor said it ran to the Pacific, and at the edge, like something provided in a fable, lay a sunken barge that had been built as a ferry. They did not bother to think. They patched up the barge and loaded their gear into it, and when the wagon train pulled out for Salt Lake City the seven bullwhackers pried themselves off the mudbank and headed downriver.

God was good to them: at least He let them live. But He kept them pretty busy. At Ashley Falls they ran their barge among the rocks and couldn't budge it. Undaunted, they made two canoes out of pine trees and lashed them together to make a kind of catamaran. When that appeared insufficient to carry their stuff, they stopped and made another.

On those cobbled craft the seven somehow got through Lodore; within it, at Disaster Falls, they found a wrecked skiff and a note on a tree saying that their unknown predecessor was getting out to Salt Lake by land. As trackless as driftwood, which they resembled, they floated through

Whirlpool and Split Mountain and into the Uinta Valley, and through and on through Desolation and Gray canyons to about the site of modern Greenriver, Utah. Their taste for river voyaging was somewhat dampened, but their ignorance of geography—in which they were not alone in 1849—might even then have persuaded them to risk the river trail farther if the Ute chief Walkara, or Walker, had not taken pity on the misguided Mericats and talked them too into going overland to Salt Lake City, there to catch on with another wagon train. Their story was told many years later by one of their number, W. L. Manly, in a book called *Death Valley in '49*.

So except for the healed or rotted inscription in the cottonwood on its southern boundary, and the name of Ashley just outside its northern prong, Dinosaur had no recorded white history until past the middle of the nineteenth century. Escalante's discoveries had leaked into American consciousness indirectly, by way of Baron von Humboldt's 1810 map of New Spain, which was based partly on the map made by Escalante's companion Miera. But nobody had heard of Ashley or Manly, and it was reserved for the third man through the canyons to be their effective discoverer. He came with no other purpose than to know; he was in search of *this* country, not on his way somewhere else.

On May 12, 1869, the first transcontinental railroad train crossed the Green at Green River, Wyoming Territory, and the first period of Western history was over. And as they crossed, the first transcontinental tourists reclining in the palace cars exchanged waves with the last continental explorers, who were calking their boats below the bridge. Those last explorers were Major John Wesley Powell's Colorado River Exploring Expedition, and they were not only closing one phase of the West but opening another. This one-armed veteran of the Union army, preparing his ten men and four boats for a raid on the unknown canyons, was later to have a greater effect on the development of the West than any other man.

He was probably, as Otis Marston points out in his story of Green River boating elsewhere in this book, not an especially good whitewater man; and, more than that, he was the first, so far as he knew. Though he had all the available information, including maps, he did not have much. He ran almost as blind as Ashley had, through a country still patched with guesswork and rumor. Though he saw Ashley's inscription in Red Canyon, he

Major John Wesley Powell, the one-armed Civil War veteran who explored much of the West and named such places as Canyon of Lodore, Echo Park, and Disaster Falls. The tale of his 1869 trip from Flaming Gorge to the Grand Canyon, *Canyons of the Colorado*, "remains one of the great Western adventure stories."

Pat Lynch, a hermit who settled in Echo Park sometime in the 1870s. Kolb Collection, Northern Arizona University.

had no idea who Ashley was, and he misread the date as 1855 and guessed that Ashley must have been a prospector.

Powell was not the first explorer of these canyons; but he was the first explorer who "took." He brought the arts of written record along with him, he measured and mapped as he went, he left a trail that led backward into the broad migration track of western civilization. Working his four heavy, awkward, overloaded boats laboriously down and over and around rapids and falls, he named what he passed, and behind him the canyons stretched northward to the railroad, forever now a part of human knowledge.

He passed and misread Ashley's daub, passed Brown's Park (then called Brown's Hole) with its tracks of Indian and fur-trader and rustler and horse thief and its ruins of old Fort Davy Crockett, earlier called Fort Misery, left over from fur-trade days. Once he dropped through the Gate of Lodore, which is for practical purposes the northern river entrance to the present Monument, the map and its names are his: the Canyon of Lodore, Disaster Falls, where he lost a boat, Triplet Falls, Hell's Half Mile, Echo Park, Whirlpool Canyon and Island Park and Split Mountain. The accounts written by himself and the men of his party for various newspapers were the first reports on that country, except for Jim Beckwourth's monumental lies, that the world at large saw. The photographs taken by his photographers E. O. Beaman and Jack Hillers in the next few years were the first pictorial record, and brought the canyons to the parlor stereoscopes of the nation. Powell's own *Report on the Exploration of the Colorado River of the West* remains one of the great Western adventure stories, as well as a cornerstone of early geology.

The Major hung on to this country which he had opened. He ran the canyons again in 1871, and he was exploring the area by land all through the seventies. He clarified the whole region of the Plateau Province, stretching all the way from Wyoming to modern Lake Mead, and in person or through his collaborators he gave it not merely a map and names, but much of its geological history and an explanation of its forms. Reading the rocks of this country so strange, so unstudied, and so perfectly exposed by the cutting edges of the rivers, he produced a second monograph, *The Geology of the Uinta Mountains of Utah and a Portion of Country Adjacent Thereto*, and in that book and its predecessor, the *Exploration*, laid the foundations for much of the modern science of geomorphology. In the area east and south of Dinosaur, among the White River and Uinta Utes, he began the studies of the native tribes that eventually made him, in the words of Spencer Baird of the Smithsonian, the one who "knew more about the live Indian than any live man."

The real discoverer of the Dinosaur canyons was the man who brought knowledge to them, and that man was Powell. Though Clarence King's Survey of the 40th Parallel worked across the northern edge of the Uintas in the late sixties, and both F. V. Hayden and the celebrated paleontologist Othniel C. Marsh had touched the fringes a year or two later, it was Powell who penetrated the country and made it his own. King, Hayden, and Marsh all persist on the map as names of high Uinta peaks, but Powell's mark is all over the map. He is the *genius loci* of Dinosaur, as of all the canyons of the Green and Colorado. Schoolmaster to the nation, explorer, enthusiast, planner, and prophet, he probably affected more lives in the West than any of our Presidents have, and it was from the canyons of Dinosaur that he drew much of his early knowledge and the hints that a long career would develop into policies of land and water and settlement vital to half the continent.

But it was not Major Powell who got the Dinosaur canyons preserved as part of the National Park System, and not he who gave the Monument its somewhat misleading name. That, or the beginning of it, was the work of another enthusiast, less illustrious but quite as dedicated, named Earl Douglass.

DOUGLASS, like Powell, was a frontier farm boy, self-made, partly self-educated. When he came into the Uinta Valley he was already a distinguished field geologist, paleontologist, and botanist. He had worked with Marsh at Yale and botanized with C. G. Pringle in Mexico; he had discovered the mammalian fossils that dated the controversial Fort Union deposits in Montana; he was the discoverer of the duckbill dinosaur, and one of the first authorities in the world on Tertiary mammals. He first conducted a search through the Uinta Valley because a hunch told him that giant bones reported by sheepherders meant a real deposit, a regular dinosaur quarry, somewhere near. And he was encouraged in his bone-hunting by Andrew Carnegie, who sent him out on a personal commission to find things to fill the Carnegie Museum's Hall of Vertebrate Paleontology in Pittsburgh, and win people to education with something as big as a barn.

Douglass found his dinosaur deposit in August 1909, when he stumbled across a row of Brontosaur vertebræ weathered out in relief in an exposed wall of the Morrison formation[1] below the mouth of Split Mountain Canyon. He worked the quarry under the most primitive conditions for fifteen years, scraping and blasting and chiseling at the rock, removing and labeling the bones, packing them in homemade plaster of paris cooked out of the local gypsum ledges, hauling them to the railroad dozens of miles

---

1 See Table of Rock Strata, p. 30.

away and shipping them back to the Carnegie Institute—700,000 pounds of them altogether.

He filled not only Carnegie's hall but many another; in almost any good paleontological museum the world around you are likely to encounter the bones of dinosaurs, big or little, carnivorous or herbivorous, that were grounded on the Jurassic bar where Monument Headquarters now stands, and were patiently picked out of the rock 120,000,000 years later by Earl Douglass and his helpers.

In a very real way, Douglass gave his life to that dinosaur graveyard. He put his best years into it. His unfinished stone house, part of the dream he had of an irrigated homestead on the banks of the Green, still stands there with the wind lonesome through its window and door holes and the lizards alert on its sills—as eloquent an archæological monument as any the Fremont people left. Within a little fence, under homemade headstones below the dune-like Jurassic foothills of the Uintas, lie the bodies of his father and sister. These things give him a dry and whispering vested interest in the place; his innocent, laborious, enthusiastic spirit persists there.

He is also the reason why the Dinosaur Monument exists, for he found it so hard to protect his diggings from souvenir-hunters that he had to do something. At first he tried to take out a mineral claim, but found that bones, even petrified ones, were not among the minerals. So he appealed to the Carnegie Museum, and the Museum took its influence to Washington, and on October 4, 1915, Woodrow Wilson by proclamation set aside the eighty acres around the quarry as Dinosaur National Monument.

The quarry is still part of the Monument, whose headquarters building sits next door. Eventually, with funds, there will be a roofed-over natural museum in the pit, with the bones of one or several dinosaurs exposed in high relief and in place, and with dioramas to show the Jurassic swamp world partially and accidentally preserved across scores of millions of years.

But the dinosaur quarry which gave the Monument its name is no more than the front yard of the people's park here established. Back of this natural schoolroom, which until it can be properly developed must remain a dusty hole in the side of a sun-smitten ridge, is the living laboratory of the Green and Yampa canyons stretching all the way from the mouth of Split

Mountain to Steamboat Rock, and from that natural dividing cliff up the Yampa to Lily Park and up the Green through Lodore to Brown's Park.

The canyons were added to the Dinosaur National Monument by proclamation of Franklin D. Roosevelt on July 14, 1938, in a move which was part of the national rescue operation to save eroded range lands and mined Dust Bowl fields and endangered watersheds and half-spoiled wilderness areas from total ruin. The consciousness of national guilt and mismanagement, and the press of necessity, were strong then; they are less strong now, when partially successful rescue work and a rainier cycle have temporarily healed some of the scars of the thirties. To this moment, at least, the Green and Yampa canyons have been saved intact, a wilderness that is the property of all Americans, a 325-square-mile preserve that is part schoolroom and part playground and part—the best part—sanctuary from a world paved with concrete, jet-propelled, smog-blanketed, sterilized, over-insured, aseptic; a world mass-produced with interchangeable parts, and with every natural beautiful thing endangered by the raw engineering power of the twentieth century.

We live in the Antibiotic Age, and Antibiotic means literally "against life." We had better not be against life. That is the way to become as extinct as the dinosaurs. And if, as the population experts were guessing in November 1954, the human race will (other things being equal) have increased so much in the next three hundred years that we will have only a square yard of ground apiece to stand on, then we may want to take turns running to some preserved place such as Dinosaur. *How much wilderness do the wilderness-lovers want?* ask those who would mine and dig and cut and dam in such sanctuary spots as these. The answer is easy: *Enough so that there will be in the years ahead a little relief, a little quiet, a little relaxation, for any of our increasing millions who need and want it.* That means we need as much wilderness as can still be saved. There isn't much left, and there is no more where the old open spaces came from.

Perhaps, when the Jurassic equivalent of a hornet stung a dinosaur somewhere out along his eighty or ninety feet of tail, it may have taken him ten or fifteen minutes to get the word. Even when he had a regional organization, the so-called "second brain" of the Stegosaurus, he was mentally retarded; his reactions were slow, with results that we can read in the rocks of the quarry in Dinosaur National Monument. It should not take us so long as it took Stegosaurus to get word that is vital to us. There is some evidence already that we run the risk of an over-specialization as fatal as that of the sauropods—we may over-engineer ourselves. The vital wilderness, the essential hoarded living-space, the open and the green and the quiet, might not survive the bulldozer as readily as they survived Ashley's bullboats and Manly's bullwhackers.

A place is nothing in itself. It has no meaning, it can hardly be said to exist, except in terms of human perception, use, and response. The wealth and resources and usefulness of any region are only inert potential until man's hands and brain have gone to work; and natural beauty is nothing until it comes to the eye of the beholder. The natural world, actually, is the test by which each man proves himself: I see, I feel, I love, I use, I alter, I appropriate, therefore I am. Or the natural world is a screen onto which we project our own images; without our images there, it is as blank as the cold screen of an empty movie house. We cannot even describe a place except in terms of its human uses.

And as the essential history of Dinosaur is its human history, the only possible destruction of Dinosaur will be a human destruction. Admittedly it would be idiotic to preach conservation of such a wilderness in perpetuity, just to keep it safe from all human use. It is only for human use that it has any meaning, or is worth preserving. But there is a vast difference among uses. Some uses use things *up* and some last forever. Recreation, properly controlled, is a perpetual use, and a vital one. It is possible to make such a wilderness as Dinosaur accessible without ruining it, and more than possible that its value for human relief from twentieth-century strains and smells and noises will prove greater than its problematic, limited, and short-term value for water or power, especially when those values can be had at other sites without violating this unique and beautiful canyon sanctuary.

We have learned something of what we risk when we mess around with nature's balances. If we destroy even so apparently worthless and harmful an item as down timber in a forest, we destroy the home of insects and grubs that are the food of certain birds. Destroying their food, we drive the birds out or thin them out, and in doing so we remove one of the principal policing agents. Deprived of its winged police, our nice cleaned-up forest

Powerful

may be infected with sudden devastating pests, more virulent and less controllable than anything that nature's checks and balances have permitted before.

Eventually we may learn that it is quite as dangerous to remake without sufficient precaution the total face of the planet, to turn our bulldozers and earthmovers loose just because we *can*.

Back in the canyons of the Green and Yampa, and in the pockets alongside streams, there have been hermits and squatters and isolated ranchers from the 1870's on. One of them, old Pat Lynch, heard about Echo Park from his friend Major Powell and settled there probably in the seventies. During many years in the canyons he spread himself; he was a one-man Occupation of what was called locally Pat's Hole. He had cabins and cave shelters in both Echo Park and Castle Park; a cave on the Rial Chew ranch on Pool Creek still contains some of his personal belongings and his sapling bed. Castle Park seems to have been the real Pat's Hole, headquarters of Pat's occupation, for in the possession of Charley Mantle is a notice which says: "To all who this may consarn that I Pat Lynch do lay claim on this botom for my home and support   Wrote the 8th month of 1886 by P L ynch."

Pat was the first white man to use the Yampa and Green river canyons, and he used them both for his livelihood and for his pleasure. He did not neglect immortality: his private petroglyph, a ship under full sail, is pecked into the cliff in Castle Park to link his spirit with Fremont man and Ute and Spaniard and fur-trade partisan. He was a cultural horizon: University of Colorado archæologists excavating Hell's Midden found a whole clearly defined layer, already covered with silt and dirt, containing the suspender buttons, cartridge cases, and other artifacts and relics of Pat Lynch's authentic life.

But the most characteristic of the remains he left is one that might be used as a motto by all the increasing users of the canyons who have come after him. In a cave that had been one of Pat's shelters, the Mantles found a note. It said, in the brogue that cropped out even in Pat's writing:

If in those caverns you shelter take Plais do to them no harm Lave everything you find around hanging up or on the ground.

That is all conservation is about. That is all the National Parks are about. Use, but do no harm.

It is legitimate to hope that there may left in Dinosaur the special kind of human mark, the special record of human passage, that distinguishes man from all other species. It is rare enough among men, impossible to any other form of life. *It is simply the deliberate and chosen refusal to make any marks at all.* Sometimes we have withheld our power to destroy, and have left a threatened species like the buffalo, a threatened beauty spot like Yosemite or Yellowstone or Dinosaur, scrupulously alone. We are the most dangerous species of life on the planet, and every other species, even the earth itself, has cause to fear our power to exterminate. But we are also the only species which, when it chooses to do so, will go to great effort to save what it might destroy.

It is a better world with some buffalo left in it, a richer world with some gorgeous canyons unmarred by signboards, hot-dog stands, super highways, or high-tension lines, undrowned by power or irrigation reservoirs. If we preserved as parks only those places that have no economic possibilities, we would have no parks. And in the decades to come, it will not be only the buffalo and the trumpeter swan who need sanctuaries. Our own species is going to need them too.

It needs them now.

other needs we have as humans

Geological Exhibit*

Eliot Blackwelder

ANY PERSON of normal curiosity, visiting the Dinosaur region for the first time, is almost sure to ask himself how all its strange and interesting features were made, and why they are here rather than somewhere else. Why do we find flat-topped mesas in one locality and sharp hogback ridges in another? Why are some of the canyon sides a series of vertical cliffs and gently sloping terraces, while others are merely steep, without terraces? Why should a river like the Green, leaving a wide open valley in Island Park, dive into a rocky canyon cut almost lengthwise through what is aptly called Split Mountain?

These questions intrigued some of the early explorers of the region, particularly such well-known geologists as Hayden and Powell. In the course of several seasons devoted to the exploration of the Colorado River and its tributaries, Powell found the region a peculiarly favorable place to analyze the complex facts about erosion, and he worked out many of the principles which govern the formation of these distinctive features. He is therefore remembered as one of the most important contributors to that branch of the science of geology which has long been called *physiography*, and more recently *geomorphology*.

---

* The information in this section was up to date when this book was first written, but current geology is different from that noted here.

These men soon perceived that each cliff along the canyon wall corresponded exactly to a bed of relatively hard rock such as sandstone or massive limestone, and that the height of the cliff always matched the thickness of the layer. It soon became plain that the verticality of the cliffs was the result of the intersecting vertical cracks caused by the bending and warping which the region had suffered in much earlier times. As the underlying bed of soft shale is worn away by water and wind, the brittle, fractured layer of hard rock is undermined, so that individual blocks break off and roll down into the river one by one. The cliff itself thus recedes, though it maintains its vertical face; and no matter how much a canyon widens, its walls will retain their characteristic profile.

Wherever a long, narrow ridge appeared, like those near the dinosaur quarry, examination showed that it matched closely the location of one of the harder strata bent up in an inclined position along the flank of one of the great folds. Since the cracks in the hard layers generally stand at right angles to the stratum itself, these hogbacks have inclined cliffs, if they have any at all, rather than vertical ones.

On the other hand, Powell observed that broad open valleys had been excavated out of shale or other soft rocks, and that the shape of the lowland, whether round or elongated, corresponded exactly to the surface distribution of such rocks. Likewise, on the walls of the canyons, whenever a bed of shale was sandwiched in between the harder cliff-forming layers, it formed a gently sloping shelf exactly corresponding to the thickness of the bed.

But there were other features which could not be explained merely by differences in hardness of the rock, or differences in the altitude of the beds or the forms of their outcrops. Geologists noted that along the summit of the Uinta Mountains, which now rise into a cold sub-arctic climate, the crest was marked by ragged peaks with spacious alcoves in the heads of the lateral valleys—features made by the action of large glaciers which were prevalent there not more than ten thousand years ago. Farther down, in the forest-clad belt, the valleys tended to be V-shaped, while the ridges between them were rounded and the cliffs along their sides were less marked, partly because they were somewhat masked with soil and vegetation. In that zone the climate favors the growth of plant life, which in turn protects from erosion the soil that develops very slowly from the decay of the underlying rocks.

In the lowest parts of the district, which had a hotter and drier climate, the forest was absent, and the scattered shrubs and bunch grass afforded a much less effective cover for the soil. In times of exceptionally heavy rains, copious rills descending over such slopes developed great erosive power and rapidly dug ravines in the weaker rocks. In severe cases all the soil was swept away, leaving the rocks fully exposed. Even the wind plays a part in denuding such unprotected areas.

On some of the steepest slopes, particularly where the rocks occur in thin beds or are much fractured, a special type of erosion becomes dominant. Angular rubble, even large blocks and boulders, dislodged by the wasting of the cliffs, rolls down the steep declivities, rasping and gouging the softer rocks as it goes. By this process of dry-rubble erosion, round-bottomed chutes are formed with sharpened ridges between them.

From studies such as those made by Powell and his followers, physiographers have come to realize that the size, shape, and erodability of various rock masses, the various processes of erosion (which in turn are dictated largely by climate), and the length of time during which the various conditions have continued, are the things that determine the nature of the individual features of any landscape. There are few places in our country which afford a greater variety of conditions than Dinosaur National Monument, or a better opportunity to study the work of these geologic agents.

Major Powell and other early physiographers, while exploring this region of the Green River valley, worked out the essential principles of what geologists now call the "cycle of erosion." They understood that any region which remains stable—free from interference by earth movements—will eventually be worn down by streams and other surface agents to an almost featureless plain. They realized that the process would be slow and that the final stage would be the slowest of all, because the sluggish streams would have little power. They were aware that the removal of masses of hard rock would lag behind the rest of the process, and so those masses would come to stand out as low mountains and hills, and where they occurred in the channels of the streams would form rapids and falls. They pointed out that each individual stream, using sand and gravel as abrasives, tended to cut its channel downward until it had a smooth and very gentle profile from its headwaters to its mouth, with only enough fall to give the stream enough power to flow and to carry the material delivered into it. A river of that sort has a gradient of less than one foot per mile in its lower course, whereas Green River, still cutting through the hard quartz-ites in the Canyon of Lodore, makes an average descent of nearly twenty feet per mile. No stream is satisfied until it has cut its channel down to that smooth line and has removed all rapids and other obstacles in its course. Also, no stream can erode its bed below that profile.

In the later stages of this cycle streams develop horizontal curves, even serpentine courses, eroding sidewards and thus widening the bottoms of their valleys. The early explorers soon realized that the devious courses of such canyons as that of the lower Yampa must have been inherited from a time when the river meandered upon a wide plain, and that the pattern was incised deeply into the rock as the whole region was later uplifted. Canyons of this sort are often called "entrenched meanders."

Not quite all the conclusions reached by Powell and his associates in the early days of exploration have withstood the closer scrutiny of later geologists. To account for the remarkable course of the Green River, which attacks and pierces the range in a deep canyon instead of skirting the eastern end of the Uinta Mountains and thus finding its way to the lowland of the Uinta Valley to the south, Powell suggested that the river had developed its course on an earlier plain, and that the long Uinta arch had been squeezed up beneath it so slowly that the stream was able to maintain its channel by sawing a canyon across the rising fold. While this has probably happened in various parts of the world, the available facts indicate that Green River developed millions of years after the great Uinta fold was made.

Corrected by later scientists or not, Powell and his co-workers in these canyons made notable contributions to knowledge. They could not help doing so, for the canyons of the West, and these canyons of the Green and Yampa among the most notable of them, afford opportunities equaled only in a few places on the globe for the study of earth history and the forces that have made the world as we know it. It is not everywhere that we are privileged to look into the very heart of a mountain.

And so it is plain that there is more to looking at a canyon or a mountain than merely filling the eye with scenery. The more we know about canyons and cliffs, buttes and ridges, valleys and terraces—their origin and their structure and the history of the strata that compose them—the more satisfying the scenery itself becomes. The further our curiosity probes back into the story of the rocks, openly revealed but in a language strange to most of us, the further our imagination is stretched by new revelations, and by a new concept of time. What has been the history of Dinosaur through the tens of millions of years of which we have some record?

North America seems so stable and unchanging that most of us find it difficult to realize that none of its familiar features have existed for more than a fraction of the known history of the Earth, which stretches back more than two billion years. A few hundred thousand years ago the Great Lakes did not exist. Hardly more than ten million years back there was no Yosemite Valley in the Sierra Nevada: that part of the range was then occupied in part by a string of active volcanoes subject to violent eruptions. Once, about seventy-five million years earlier, the Gulf of Mexico spread northward over all the Great Plains, and joined with the Arctic Ocean, which advanced southward to meet it. Equally striking changes have repeatedly affected all the rest of our continent.

The present aspect of the part of Colorado and Utah with which this book is concerned is the product of a geologic history covering many hundreds of millions of years. From conditions utterly unlike those which now exist, the region has acquired its present features only very gradually. Where high mountains now rise, low plains or even a broad sea bottom once spread; and there were in earlier times imposing mountain ranges where today we see only lowlands. Part of the time the region was covered by an extension of the Gulf of Mexico; at other times a wide arm of the Pacific extended in over it from the west.

Equally great changes have taken place in the climate and in the plant and animal life of the region. Instead of the cool semi-arid conditions of today, there have been long periods when the climate was essentially tropical and the land was covered with luxuriant vegetation in which the dinosaurs and the animals upon which some of them preyed found favorable conditions for their existence.

Going back in history about six hundred million years, to the Pre-Cambrian era, we find clear evidence that the Utah region was then a plain over which rivers from adjacent mountains were spreading copious layers of sand and mud. The surface of the earth in that vicinity and time must have been slowly sinking, for the accumulation of these sedimentary layers continued until they were more than two miles thick. The red-brown color of these deposits indicates that they were formed under a warm climate with well-marked rainy and dry seasons — conditions much like those of parts of northwestern India today. In the course of time the beds of reddish deposits became consolidated into hard rocks which we now call sandstone (or quartzite) and some shale. The change into rock was brought about largely by the chemical action of water deep underground depositing natural cement among the grains. We can now see these deposits as successive layers of brown rock (the Uinta Quartzite) in the great cliffs of the Canyon of Lodore, and in the peaks along the axis of the great Uinta Range to the northwest. They are exposed even in the depths of Split Mountain Canyon.

Millions of years later, in the Cambrian period, slow movement inside the earth raised the district sufficiently above sea level so that river deposition ceased and the streams were enabled to excavate valleys out of the upper portion of the ancient river plain. The floors of these valleys were slowly widened until they merged into a single broad plain of erosion, which was underlain by the brown sandstones and shales made long before. To complete such a plain of erosion ordinarily requires some millions of years; to such a plain any region, however mountainous, will eventually come if the forces inside the Earth cease to disturb it for a sufficiently long while.

Thereafter, as the exceedingly slow warping of the solid earth was resumed, the region was again slowly lowered. Erosion then ceased, and gravel, sand, and silt began to be deposited once more. But this time the subsidence went farther, carrying the Dinosaur region well below sea level and allowing an arm of the ocean, probably the Pacific, to spread over much of the western United States. As a result, the river deposits which formed the surface of the country were overlaid by layers of other material, such as accumulates on sea floors, where the currents redistribute the fine sand and mud swept into the ocean from the land.

As the sea became more and more extensive, and the land areas available for erosion became fewer and farther away from the Dinosaur area, the supply of land-derived material dwindled to almost nothing. In place of it the sea floor gradually was covered with a chalk-like deposit composed of the shells and other hard parts of myriads of plants and animals which lived in the sea. For the most part these were almost microscopic in size, yet in due time, during long burial, these layers were consolidated into limestone such as the Madison Limestone of Mississippian age which forms the imposing cliffs in Lodore. That particular bed of limestone has all the characteristics of a deposit made in deep water, probably more than a thousand feet deep.

For nearly five hundred million years these two processes alternated— the deposition of sedimentary material either on plains or sea floors, and the erosion of an uplifted land area into resulting plains of erosion. Geologists customarily divide this immensely long time into periods and epochs to which they have given such names as Cambrian, Devonian, and Jurassic, each of them many millions of years long. For those who have the necessary time and interest, the record is visible in the rocks which form the walls of the picturesque canyons of the Dinosaur National Monument. That the periods of deposition predominated over the periods of erosion is shown by the thick sequence of rock layers still remaining. The present period is of course one of erosion.

From the nature and color of the remaining strata and the fossil plants and animals which they reveal, it is evident that the prevailing conditions changed from time to time. The climate was more often tropical or sub-tropical than cool. Periods of abundant rainfall, of monsoon climate, or of severe aridity alternated, each lasting for millions of years. There were also important variations in the depth of that part of the sea.

At the close of the Cretaceous period, about sixty million years ago, there occurred a major event that left its mark on a broad strip of North America extending from Alaska south through Mexico. Powerful forces within the Earth slowly compressed the continent from west to east to such an extent that the outer crust, to a thickness of several miles, was wrinkled into long folds, and the whole belt bulged up many thousands of feet above sea level. The rock strata were not only folded, but extensively cracked and dislocated. Although subsequent erosion has largely demolished these wrinkles and fault scarps, their roots remain, and can easily be traced in the canyons of the Green River and its tributaries. An airplane flight over the region also discloses them in the pattern of the curved outcrops of distinctive rock layers. One of the most conspicuous of these

talking about rocks and time period

23

broad folds trends east and west in the Uinta Range, while minor folds and some large faults interrupt its flanks.

It has been clearly established that any deformative Earth movement of this kind takes place so slowly that the whole episode lasts millions of years. It would be almost imperceptible to anyone living there at the time. Meanwhile, rock decay and erosion set in and busily wear down the mountains even while they are rising. If the great Uinta arch had been formed quickly and in recent times, it would now be a range about the height of Mount Everest. However, it probably never reached any such altitude in its continual struggle against the erosive power of streams, landslides, glaciers, and other destructive agents.

The waste products of erosion—mostly mud and sand, with minor amounts of gravel—were swept down into the broad basins between the folds or were carried out to the oceans. These deposits of the Eocene epoch accumulated to depths of thousands of feet and spread far up over the flanks of the subdued mountain ranges. Both north and south of the Uinta fold, large lakes existed for long periods of time, as is now attested by thick layers of clay-shale containing fossil freshwater fishes. From the plant leaves locally preserved in these shales it is evident that the climate was sub-tropical and moist. One of the most interesting and economically important of these deposits is the oil shale, which is so rich in a wax-like residue of dead organic matter that oil can be readily distilled from the rock. The most extensive of the oil-shale beds lies in Colorado, southeast of the Dinosaur Monument. In the future, after ordinary supplies of petroleum have been depleted, that district is likely to yield oil and gasoline on a large scale for many decades.

The final result of all this Eocene deposition was that by the close of the period, perhaps forty million years ago, the Utah-Colorado region was again a series of alluvial plains, among which only low remnants of the once-great mountain chains rose here and there. By that time the landscape may have looked somewhat like parts of present-day southwestern Arizona.

In the ensuing period, the Oligocene, the Rocky Mountain belt was again slowly uplifted, but this time with less horizontal compression and hence only gentle folding. Increased altitude again gave power to the streams, which rapidly cut their channels down through the Eocene deposits, still relatively soft, and into the older rocks below. The first result must have been a series of narrow canyons. As streams are able to erode soft rocks like shale far more rapidly than the harder ones, they excavated broad open valleys, such as Brown's Park, in the areas underlain by softer strata. Elsewhere the streams were still engaged in slowly carving narrow slots through the massive harder rocks.

In the Pliocene period, less than ten million years ago, a reversal of stream behavior from erosion to deposition induced the gradual filling of the broad valleys and basins with gravel and sand. A few beds of volcanic ash, now inter-layered with the river-laid sand, afford a record of eruptions in some near-by region, not yet identified, from which the wind drifted the dust over a wide area. The change in stream behavior may have been caused by a general subsidence of the region and also by a change to an arid climate. There is good evidence that about this time the lifting of the high mountain ranges along the Pacific coast raised a more effective barrier

View of Rainbow and Island Park from Split Mountain.

Tilted strata on the flanks of Split Mountain.

The meanders of the Green River through Island Park.

These two views of Mitten Park Fault, from Harpers Corner (*above*) and the Green River (*left*), demonstrate the warping and lifting of rock strata that so characterize the faults of Dinosaur National Monument.

In Castle Park and below, the Yampa River cuts a tortuous course through high sandstone cliffs.

against the moisture-laden winds from the ocean, as they now do for the desert of southeastern California. In the area of Brown's Park, just north of the Monument, the white sandy deposits were built up under these conditions to a thickness of more than twelve hundred feet, perhaps enough to bury some of the lower mountain ridges.

We have no reason to believe that the Colorado River system was in existence before this time. When the epoch of arid climate gave way to more moist conditions, lakes may have formed in the desert basins and spilled over the lowest point in the rim of each, the integrated river thus reaching the Gulf of California step by step. The outlets of the several lakes would cut notches in the rims of the basins and may well, in this way, have drained all the lakes. In this process the Green River and its tributaries probably established their courses on the alluvial deposits.

Even before this latest epoch of widespread deposition came to an end, Earth movements became more active again, slowly warping or raising the surface and producing a number of faults which trend roughly parallel to the Uinta Range.

From that time to the present the entire Rocky Mountain region has risen slowly and intermittently by as much as 8,000 to 10,000 feet. This elevation has greatly increased the erosive power of the streams as well as the supply of water draining into them from the higher mountains. As a result the rivers have again cut deep canyons in the harder rocks and more spacious valleys in the softer ones. The meandering courses which they developed on the alluvial plains of the Pliocene epoch are now found reflected in the serpentine courses of some of the modern canyons such as those of the lower Yampa: for an established river beneath which the land is rising cuts deeper into the land like a buzz-saw into a log pushed against it.

During the last million years or more (the Pleistocene epoch) several marked climatic variations have taken place, and each has left its mark upon the landscape. Although through most of the period it was slightly warmer than at present, there were several episodes of much colder climate lasting some thousands of years each. The changes apparently affected the entire globe. During these cold epochs large glaciers developed in the canyons on both sides of the Uinta Range, and there left moraines which are easily recognized today. Farther down Green River and its tributaries, in open spaces such as that around Jensen, Utah, the copious supply of gravel and sand poured into the streams by the active glaciers can be traced southward for long distances, appearing at intervals in terraces 50 to 250 feet high along either side of the river. During the glacial and interglacial stages the zones of vegetation, such as the forest and sagebrush zones, slowly moved downward and then upward again several thousand feet in response to variations in the average temperature. Meanwhile the slow deepening of the canyons themselves continued; it is still far short of completion.

All this is implied or explicitly told in the geological exhibit called Dinosaur. This is the story to which every flash flood and every landslide contributes, each according to clear natural law. And this is what we hear and see when we stand at the edge of Hell's Half Mile or Moonshine Rapid and look and listen as the buckskin water of the spring runoff pounds and flashes past. We are watching the canyons deepened; we are hearing the earth remade.

TABLE OF ROCK STRATA
IN DINOSAUR MONUMENT AND VICINITY
(*Age in millions of years, estimated*)

PERIODS	FORMATION NAMES	THICKNESS IN FEET	CHARACTER OF STRATA	AGE
Pleistocene and Recent	Alluvium	0–50	River gravel and sand on terraces and flood plains.	0–1
Pliocene	Brown's Park	1,200	Sandstone, white to gray, rather soft. A few beds of white volcanic ash. Local conglomerate at the base.	4–6
Cretaceous	Mancos	5,000	Dark-gray marine shale with lenses of sandstone.	
	Frontier	200	Sandstone, dark shale and coal.	
	Mowry	125	Dark-gray marine shale with abundant fish scales.	70–85
	Dakota	100	Yellowish sandstone and conglomerate with beds of gray and red shale. Some fossil wood.	
Jurassic	Morrison	750	Varicolored shale and sandstone with some conglomerate. Contains fossil wood, shells, and dinosaur bones. Stream and lake deposits.	
	Curtis	260	Gray sandstone, shale, and limestone. Marine.	
	Entrada	165	Gray, buff, and pink sandstone. Probably a wind deposit on land.	135–165
	Carmel	125	Red shale and siltstone with beds of gypsum.	
	Navajo	700	Buff to red cross-bedded sandstone. Deposited largely by wind.	
Triassic	Chinle	230	Red shale and siltstone with some sandstone. Teeth and bones of reptiles. Stream deposits.	
	Shinarump	50	Coarse sandstone and conglomerate. Yellowish. River deposit.	165–200
	Moenkopi	800	Red shale and sandstone with ripple marks. Non-marine.	

whats been around and the time
thats alot time
Context/period of time

TABLE OF ROCK STRATA
IN DINOSAUR MONUMENT AND VICINITY (*continued*)

PERIODS	FORMATION NAMES	THICKNESS IN FEET	CHARACTER OF STRATA	AGE
Permian	Park City	50	Thin-bedded limestone with some sandstone and shale. Marine.	210–220
Carboniferous	Weber	1,000	Light-gray cross-bedded sandstone.	
	Morgan	1,280	Interbedded gray limestone, white and reddish sandstone, and limy shale. Marine.	
	(Transitional)	185	Black shale with white and buff sandstone below. Non-marine.	250-300
	Madison	600	Massive buff to dark-gray limestone, containing a few marine shells, and corals.	
*				
Cambrian	Lodore	400	Coarse white and reddish sandstone with a few beds of shale. Partly marine.	430–440
Pre-Cambrian	Uinta Mts.	12,000	Coarse red to white quartzite or 550-700 sandstone with some conglomerate and thin beds of shale.	550–700

* *In this area the Ordovician, Silurian, and Devonian periods are apparently not represented by sedimentary deposits.*

The Natural World of Dinosaur

Olaus Murie and Joseph W. Penfold

WILDLIFE, and the natural world it depends upon, is an important part of Dinosaur's superb canyon country, as important as Steamboat Rock, the Great Overhang, Castle Park, or even the living Green and Yampa rivers. Wildlife with an integrity of its own, achieved through countless eons of time, is part of the area's integrity, part of the unity which the Park System is designed to preserve. More than any other aspect of the Monument, the living things give present-day continuity to forces beyond our comprehension. Just as the rivers are alive, constantly carving their channels, so the wildlife helps us to appreciate that the area is no spot in time quick-frozen for our entertainment, but rather a continuing evolution of which we too are an inescapable part.

Certainly the living things bridge for us the gap between ourselves and the prehistoric people whose pictographs and petroglyphs endure on the rock. Those people saw them too, and doubtless respected them as fellow creatures. For us, they add immeasurably to the pleasure and instructiveness of the Monument.

A man cannot camp across the river from Steamboat, be awakened in the pre-dawn gray by Canadian honkers flying back and forth the length of the rock as if to hear their cries echo and reverberate, and then tell himself that these fine birds are measurable only as so many hours of sport and so many pounds of meat. Nor can he see a fork-horn buck trot downstream ahead of his raft, splash through shallows and along beaches, and stop behind a screen of juniper to watch the raft drift by, and then ring up that mule deer's value as just one more potential point in the state's hunter-success ratio. There is hardly a visitor to the serene natural world of these canyons who does not think, on hearing a coyote's outcast howl from the bench or seeing a cat's pug track in the dust, that these creatures too belong, and are a necessary part of what he came here to see and know.

The wildlife of Dinosaur is not to be evaluated in terms of numbers, hunting-licenses purchased, guides employed, sporting-equipment manufactured, or man-days spent in the field with rod or gun. These measurements, valid elsewhere, do not apply to our national parks. Here wildlife is not merely tolerated or promoted as a harvestable resource: it belongs. On the other hand, Dinosaur Monument is not a biotic whole for many species—it does not provide the year-round conditions of life—and from time to time artificial controls may be necessary to preserve the species and the habitat on which it depends. No technician who has ever reported on the Dinosaur area has failed to comment on the tragic overuse of grasses, shrubs, and plants of all types by domestic livestock over the past half-century, and this overgrazing limits the opportunity for wildlife dependent on the same rangelands.

THE SPECIES THAT HAVE GONE

The form of wildlife for which Dinosaur National Monument was named has been extinct for a million centuries. The twentieth-century visitor may not expect to photograph a forty-ton Diplodocus feeding in the shallows of Island Park, nor is he likely to be awakened in camp by a Thecondatia gnawing the grease off his frying-pan. Nevertheless, the fossils of plant and animal life that existed a hundred million years ago can help us to understand the inexorable forces of nature that produce and destroy species and that have created the cliffs and canyons and rock strata as we see them today.

While evidences of fossil deposits in the Uintas had been known since 1882, their concentration in the present quarry area was not discovered until 1909 by Earl Douglass. From then until 1922 collecting was carried on by the Carnegie Museum of Pittsburgh. Additional collecting has been done since under the auspices of the American Museum of Natural History, the United States National Museum, and the University of Utah.

As of early 1955, funds for the proper display of fossil remains in the Monument "museum" have never been available, and there is only a modest display of bones in place at the quarry. Although a tiny staff, having practically nothing to work with, has done a commendable job, the present-day visitor often leaves the quarry disappointed. Future years may see the utilization of the almost endless opportunities for an intensely interesting series of displays and interpretive programs.

Geologists tell us that the concentration of fossils at the quarry resulted from deposit of carcasses washed down some ancient stream, long before there was a Green River or anything resembling the present topography of the region, and caught on a bar, where they were covered with silt carried by the same stream. Through geological processes these layers of silt, sand, and marl became the stratum of rock known as the Morrison Formation, and within them are preserved in fossil form dinosaur bones, wood, and fresh-water shells.

The popular idea of dinosaurs is not altogether an accurate one. Dinosaurs included a large group of reptiles of a wide variety of amazing shapes and sizes, some as small as a chicken and some ninety feet long and weighing fifty tons. Of five main sub-groups, all but the Crocodilia have been extinct for at least sixty million years. The crocodiles and alligators of today provide us with a direct link to the ancient Age of Reptiles, but neither of these modern "dinosaurs" frequents the area today, nor are conditions today anything like the swampy moist world in which the ancient dinosaurs lived. That world in fossils shows us no flowering plants, but it did have ferns, horsetails, club mosses, cycads, gingkoes, and conifers, and its animals included, besides the dominant reptiles, fresh-water mussels, tortoises, and a small, primitive mammal no larger than a rat.

Between the Age of Reptiles and the historical period, Dinosaur has no link. Fragmentary evidence left by prehistoric Indians suggests that the wildlife complex of their times, as far back as three thousand years, differed little from what we know today, though further investigation of animal material associated with the Fremont people may throw further light on the wildlife of the past, and on its relationship to the early Indians.

The present animal inhabitants of Dinosaur are thus reflections of the immediate past. Some species are largely eliminated, some others have been added—principally domestic animals, whose introduction and husbandry have profoundly affected the wildlife.

ANIMALS, PAST AND PRESENT

Attempts to reconstruct a picture of primeval wildlife conditions in the Rocky Mountain West can seldom result in anything clear-cut and definite. Elements of European influence preceded the actual coming of white men by many years. Doubtless the most disrupting of these influences was the acquisition of the domesticated horse by the Indians. Made mobile by the horse and more potent by firearms, the Indians began to have much greater effect on wildlife. Moreover, explorers often disagreed in their reports of numbers and species of animals. Very likely most of them correctly documented wildlife situations they observed, but they lacked a background of knowledge of seasonal fluctuations, disturbances by hunters, including Indians, and other unknown factors.

In the same way, nowadays, one sportsman after a day's experience will report a high mountain lake fished out, while the following evening his brother Ike Walton may fill his creel in short order. Or one winter an observer will find a mountain valley alive with mule deer, and another find deer few and far between. As a result, all our evidences of primeval wildlife conditions must be cautiously used.

The archæologists' excavations demonstrate that as far back as perhaps 1500 B.C. deer, mountain sheep, bison, fox, beaver, prairie dog, marmot, rabbit, wood rat, and fish were part of the staple Indian diet. Of these species, all but the bison still persist today. The paintings and carvings on the cliffs emphasize deer and mountain sheep, suggesting that these animals were especially important to the food supply. One bird depicted, and popularly identified as a turkey, was for a while particularly interesting to bird technicians, for it indicated evidence of a much greater range for the wild turkey in these early times. Later study, however, has seemed to demonstrate that the birds pictured are cranes. The grandson of the Ute chief Colorow has stated that his grandfather told him the birds represented whooping cranes, but it seems more likely that they were sandhill cranes, which still nest in isolated spots in the region and are occasionally seen. Another game bird pictured in the Indian murals is the grouse, but whether the sage or the blue is not clear.

Both archæological remains and the scattered skulls and horn shells of historic times indicate that once the bison roamed over much of the Monument. But there is only one recorded observation of bison within the Monument boundaries—that of General Ashley, who saw several buffalo in Island Park in 1825. Even that early, however, it seems likely that bison had largely disappeared from the area. Ashley reports that several thousand Indians had camped in May 1825 in Brown's Park. That should explain why Ashley, Sage, and other explorers found no buffalo in Brown's Park, though it has since supported a sizable number of horses, cattle, and sheep. Where cattle will winter, buffalo would thrive, and so it seems logical to assume that before Indians and hunters cleaned them out, bison once inhabited pretty much the whole Monument area.

They might, in fact, be restored, if it were not for the fact that the Monument provides winter range only, and also that the region has been so consistently overgrazed that it can supply little forage. If cattle, sheep, and horses should be removed, and the vegetation given adequate opportunity to recover, the Monument might someday support a small buffalo herd, but even this would probably require fencing to prevent the animals from wandering off into other lands.

The grizzly bear is another animal which once inhabited the Monument but which must be presumed to have almost if not entirely disappeared. Warren Ferris first established the presence of "silvertips" in the area, near Vernal, Utah, in 1835. Frederick Dellenbaugh, with the second Powell expedition in 1871, saw grizzly tracks in Lodore, a short distance above Echo Park. And in 1891 Ann Willis, then thirteen years old, roped one of two grizzly cubs she encountered in Zenobia Basin. The mother bear was nearby, and charged; "Queen Ann" was rescued by cowboys, but only after her horse, as well as the mother bear, was killed. The cubs were not molested and were never reported again.

The introduction of stock-raising all but sealed the doom of these large predators, yet in Lodore Canyon in the early summer of 1954 a game-department technician found an imperfect track he believes might have been that of a grizzly. Perhaps there still exist a few individuals which have escaped man's effort to exterminate the species. Black bears also received the extermination treatment when sheep were brought in to graze the open range, but they persisted longer. A black bear cub was reported seen in Harper's Corner in 1942, and an adult was killed on Pot Creek, a few miles west of the Monument boundary, in 1948. Although there have been no authenticated reports of black bear since, some may wander into the Monument from the Uinta Mountains. However, sheepherders on privately owned lands within the Monument and on adjacent lands outside will prevent their becoming re-established.

That wolves existed in the Monument in the past is well substantiated. Cary, for example, reports large numbers in Brown's and Lily parks about the turn of the century. But about that time professional wolfers began operating there, and by 1906 there were few left. Hod Ruple, who lived at Island Park many years before and after his ranch was included within Dinosaur National Monument, saw a wolf there in 1927. A seventy-two-pound male was killed on Blue Mountain in 1942. It is probable that wolves still wander into Dinosaur, and will continue to do so as long as any remain in that part of the country and manage to escape predator-control officials.

The coyote is meagerly documented, both past and present, but that does not mean that he was ever absent from the region, or that he has entirely disappeared. The coyote has been so common that few people have troubled to record his presence or numbers. Major Powell reported that the "wolves" seen in the plains in late June, south of Split Mountain, "make the air resound with their howling after dark." Probably his wolves were coyotes. Present-day explorers of the benches and higher lands of the Monument can still hear their howling after dark, greatly diminished, to be sure, and perhaps soon to be stilled altogether through control measures on adjacent lands, including the dropping of poisoned baits from airplanes.

Dinosaur is well beyond the range assigned to the Yellowstone or Shiras moose, but at least one moose has been reported. Hod Ruple stated that he saw a moose on his Island Park ranch in 1905, but the biologist who recorded the observation thought Ruple must have been mistaken, for the country did not look at all suitable for moose. Actually, Ruple's observation is no more unusual than that of Milton Estes, who shot a moose in

Estes Park in the 1860's, or those of four other published records of moose in northern Colorado and Utah. A moose was illegally killed in the Uinta Mountains in the fall of 1954.

The scarcity of references to Yellowstone moose in the journals of explorers through lands later incorporated into the states of Wyoming, Montana, and Idaho strongly indicates that these animals were not abundant when white men first penetrated that part of the West. Their later presence in Dinosaur, and in the northern portion of Colorado and Utah, suggests that they may be extending their range. The record of Hod Ruple may thus represent a recent immigration rather than a restoration or re-invasion.

In journals of early explorers no mention occurs of North American elk (wapiti) being seen in the area now known as Dinosaur National Monument, though elk have been reported in adjacent areas and their antlers have been found within the Monument proper. Old residents state that they formerly ranged the Monument, and recent reports indicate that they may again be present.

In Warren Ferris's 1834–5 encampment on Ashley Creek, about seven miles above present-day Vernal, Utah, no elk were reported shot, but the following spring Ferris mentions elk carcasses that were cached near Ashley Gorge, presumably by some of his men, and another carcass that was buried by a grizzly bear. The abundance of deer made hunting afar unnecessary; hence elk may have been more plentiful than his diary suggests.

Rufus Sage stated seven years later that the Indians at Robidoux's Fort, in the Uinta Valley, had abundant elk skins, and there were countless numbers of these animals in Brown's Park. Yet when Wizlizenus passed through the Park in August 1839, food was very scarce, so scarce that the trader at Fort Crockett had just paid five dollars for an Indian dog. It is quite likely that had this party gone through later in the year they might have encountered numerous elk.

In the early 1900's Merritt Cary saw no evidence of elk in the Monument area, nor did he find anyone who had knowledge of elk in that region. He did learn that there were a few in the extreme northwestern corner of Colorado, and some may have persisted in the mountainous parts of the present Monument. These were not numerous, or he would have heard about them, and undoubtedly they disappeared within a few years.

Sometime later Charles Sparks, a rancher on Cold Spring Mountain just northeast of Dinosaur's present boundary, obtained some elk from Yellowstone National Park and kept them under fence for several years, later releasing them into the forest. The present elk in the Uinta Mountains also came from Yellowstone.

The small herd on Cold Spring Mountain prospered and spread into adjacent areas. In 1947 or 1948 a cow elk was reported to have wintered on a cottonwood island two miles south of Monument Headquarters. Another elk was seen on the Yampa Bench during the winter of 1952–3. Three others also apparently crossed the Monument and remained on Blue Mountain, where they were seen by several people. Probably other elk move down off the mountains in winter when there are no Park Service employees in this part of the Monument to record their movements.

Limited elk-hunting has been permitted in the eastern part of Utah for several years, and Colorado opened the Cold Spring Mountain and adjacent sections for permit hunting in 1954. As Dinosaur is principally a winter range, hunting on the fall range outside the Monument may prevent a build-up of this herd.

There is no fear of a shortage of mule deer. Dinosaur is now primarily a wintering range for deer, and no doubt always has been. Cary recorded regular deer migrations from mountains to lowlands prior to 1900, but at that time deer movements were barely perceptible because the deer were so scarce.

In the winter of 1834–5 Ferris must have encountered similar migrations, for then he found deer "as numerous as the pines and cedars among which they were found." This was not in the present Monument, but nearby; there are reasons for believing the winter deer population in the Monument would have been the same. Sage reported multitudes of deer in Brown's Park in 1842, although, as previously mentioned, Wizlizenus had earlier found no game in this basin.

The Powell expedition of 1869 secured a "fine fat deer" in Island Park, and Dellenbaugh found deer abundant in Jones Hole in 1926. In recent times Charley Mantle has seen more than a thousand in winter on the benches south of the Yampa, and Superintendent Lombard has estimated a slightly larger number along the west side of the Monument. Many persons have reported large deer populations on and around Zenobia Peak.

Rocky Mountain bighorn sheep.

Golden eagle.

Prairie falcon fledglings.

The heavy movement of mule deer into the Monument produces, in fact, an unfavorable situation. Several times in the past heavy deer mortalities have been reported, especially among fawns, which indicates insufficient forage and poor wintering conditions for such large numbers. The situation is generally true throughout the area, and is recognized by both Utah and Colorado game commissions, which have provided liberal hunting seasons to reduce populations by hunter harvest.

Research by technicians in recent years indicates that there are two separate deer migrations into the Monument, one from the Uintas to the west, wintering west of Green River, and one from the Cold Spring Mountain area to the northeast, wintering east of the Green. Visitors to the Monument will see deer in any section. While they are not numerous in the less accessible canyons, a few individuals are almost always seen by the river traveler. Close to water holes and springs in the piñon-juniper and sagebrush benches and broad high points, they can be seen by the score in the early morning, and often during the day if the hiker strikes off the roads and into the brush.

42

Perhaps the most interesting of all the "game" animals of the Monument are the bighorn sheep, which practically all the early explorers noted in their journals. William Lewis Manly, headed for the California gold fields in 1849, wrote that "on the high peaks above our heads we could see the Rocky Mountain sheep looking down defiantly at us from their mountain fastnesses, so far away that they looked no larger than jackrabbits."

Mule deer buck.

Pronghorn antelope.

Mountain lion.

Coyote.

Bus Hatch, veteran river man, recounts that in July 1915 he saw over a hundred bighorn sheep in the Pot Creek area of Lodore, thirty-five in one bunch. Later he counted but eleven in the same area. Apparently the great reduction in numbers was the result of poaching, disease, and perhaps normal cycles in their population numbers. In any event, by 1947 Superintendent Lombard was about ready to write them off as a vanished species.

Since then, however, the Colorado Game and Fish Department has made two plantings, one in Lily Park, the other in the Zenobia Peak area, totaling about forty animals. In 1954 a Game and Fish Department party encountered eight animals in the bottom of the Lodore Canyon which they believe were not transplants but vestiges of the original population.

If they are protected from poaching and from the unconscionable competition of domestic sheep for the limited forage, there is no reason why the bighorn should not build back to reasonable numbers and provide glimpses to the casual visitor of a marvelous native species in a natural, wild, and rugged setting that seems, and is, especially created for it and not duplicated elsewhere in North America.

Visitors approaching the Monument from Wyoming are likely to see pronghorn antelope, whose population has built up very fast in northwestern Colorado in recent years, partly because of protection and partly because of migrations from Wyoming, the antelope retreating southward ahead of severe blizzards. Some of them elect to remain and become residents. Undoubtedly this movement observed in recent years occurred as well in the past, and may account for fluctuations in the antelope population as reported over the past century. The photographs on the following pages show just a few of the mammals and birds that comprise the natural world of Dinosaur. While such animals as the mountain lion are reclusive and thus not likely to be observed, others—including mule deer, pronghorn antelope, and bighorn sheep—may be seen at any time along the roadways and waterways of the Monument.

Powell saw antelope on the flats south of Split Mountain. Cary relates a trapper's report that as late as 1898 thousands of individuals wintered in the region, yet in 1905 Cary found them scarce and predicted their early extinction. However, by 1945 they had increased to the point where both Utah and Colorado had limited hunting seasons in the general area.

Today, antelope are undoubtedly part-time residents of the Monument. Some of them around Lily Park are said to winter on East Cactus Flat. Eventually, when they cross Thanksgiving Gorge and find water holes on the benches, they may become permanent residents. The lands between Blue Mountain and the Yampa appear to provide suitable habitat for a small herd.

In 1951 George W. Kelly of Denver camped in Echo Park one night and woke to find the tracks of a mountain lion in the dust of the road a few yards from where he had unrolled his sleeping-bag. Earlier that year another visitor reaching Echo Park through Sand Creek Canyon caught a glimpse of a big cat high in the rocks. In this same area, the fall before, a party of visitors found lion tracks in the road, placed there between the time they had gone down the canyon and the time when they returned a few hours later. In 1952 the tracks of two lions were noted following the rim at Harper's Corner.

Mountain lions have been reported in the Monument area from earliest times. The rough terrain, with adequate food supply, has provided very favorable habitat, for the Yampa Canyon especially contains large areas where dogs cannot follow a lion and where men would find the climbing so difficult that they could easily be eluded. Nonetheless, professional hunters have taken many of them, one in 1913 taking fifteen from the area west of Lily Park.

Charley Mantle states that after forty years of ranching in Yampa Canyon he has no positive knowledge of any cattle lost to lions, though he blames lions for the loss of one colt. It seems likely that if they had caused any substantial stock losses they would have been hunted more systematically by the ranchers. Certainly one of the outstanding wildlife values of Dinosaur National Monument is the mountain-lion habitat, which affords an excellent opportunity to observe an animal fast becoming extinct elsewhere in the West. The lion's importance as a natural control for the overpopulation of deer is an added value.

Dinosaur is a home for many of the smaller animals, and in relative abundance. Up the side canyons and draws, on the benchlands, among the scattered timber, the visitor will encounter porcupine, marmot, marten, chipmunks, and squirrels. Among the rocky canyons, ledges, and outcroppings the more secretive animals travel about, occasionally to be observed: the fox, the bobcat, and the nocturnally busy pack rat.

On the sagebrush flats and gentle slopes can be seen badgers and skunks, and also the fascinating little prairie dog, doubtless doomed to extinction except in the National Park System because he competes with livestock for forage and with cultivated crops for space. Some of the native animals—the bank beaver, muskrat, and mink—live in or close to the rivers, and depend on the living streams for their home, their food, and their lives. Because they are limited to this habitat, their doings may often be watched by the river visitor who comes floating quietly downstream.

BIRDS

A catalogue of Dinosaur's birds would contain at least eighty names, though the list would not then be complete, for no winter census has ever been made.

Both the Green and Yampa rivers have a large population of the greater Canadian geese. At present the heavy nesting-areas are confined to Big Brown's Park and along the little shelves immediately adjacent to both rivers. As reported by one competent technician, "a remarkable thing is that many of these geese nest on the rocks at a considerable distance above the river. In fact, we found one nest approximately fifty feet above the river." When the goslings are developed sufficiently to swim, the adult birds are said to push them out of the nest into the water.

Ducks are common throughout the area, though it is recognized that the present nesting-habitat for all the wildfowl would be largely eliminated by reservoir flooding if dams were built at Echo Park and in Split Mountain.

Of the larger birds there are the golden eagle, an occasional bald eagle, and a variety of hawks, including the Cooper's and sparrow hawks. Smaller birds include the ruby-crowned kinglet, pine siskin, house finch, house wren, robin, chickadee, long-tailed chat, lazuli bunting, meadowlark, lark sparrow, kingbird, phœbe, mourning dove, barn swallow, cliff swallow, buzzard, crow, raven, and magpie.

FLORA

The Monument lies in an arid region where rainfall amounts to only ten to fifteen inches per year. Many species of plants have adapted themselves to the climate, however, and the altitudinal range from 4,800 feet to above 9,000—from Upper Sonoran to Canadian Zone—makes for a wide variety of growing-conditions, which in turn have encouraged an extremely varied vegetation. About 250 species of plants have been collected, and the list is by no means complete. The University of Colorado annually conducts in the Monument a field study trip for botany students.

The warm canyon bottoms grow prickly pear, sand verbena, winterfat, penstemon, tamarisk, Utah juniper, Rocky Mountain juniper, and a species of flowering currant that grows extremely large. Trees include several species of poplar (broad-leaf, narrow-leaf, aspen), along with box elder and an almost tree-like willow, and among the shrubs are a few specimens of the red-twig dogwood.

Dry hillsides have the common mountain mahogany, wax currant, service berry, and in more favorable locations antelope brush, mountain spirea, thimbleberry, mock orange, and single-leaf ash. Mormon tea, that leafless shrub with the straight green stems, as well as rabbit brush may be found at the edges of the drier places. On the truly desert flats there will be sagebrush, greasewood, saltbush, and cactus of various kinds. In Jones Hole and a few other favored valleys are found mountain maple, mountain birch, and snowberry.

One very interesting little plant classed as a shrub is occasionally found growing on cliffs, where its single taproot may run far back into a crack to find moisture. This is the spirea cæspitosa, which often forms low mats several feet long and broad that sprawl over the rocks or hang free from a cliff face.

Piñon pine and Utah juniper are the principal evergreens, but there are extensive shady slopes on which Douglas fir and some Rocky Mountain juniper are found.

In spring after the snows have melted and the ground is warmed a little, the Monument blazes out with whole slopes of spring beauties, buttercups, Mertensia, the tiny blue-eyed Mary, white candytuft, yellow violets, wild onions, and the distinctive little yellow bell or Fritilaria.

Later the red paintbrush will thrust up spots of bright color, blue larkspur will be seen in protected places, and in favorable patches of soil or moisture yellow beeplant, wallflowers, penstemon, balsamroot, Zygadenus, golden pea, small daisies, and several species of lupines will pattern the red earth with brighter color.

Some hillsides, apparently barren at first glance, will show on closer inspection an almost solid covering of beautiful pink trailing phlox in early spring, and sulphur flowers and sedums later. Especially moist places will produce the dart-like shooting star or the delicate little white flower called Tellima.

In the fall, yellow flowers predominate, mostly those of the sunflower family such as Senecios, true sunflowers, gumweed, and goldenrod, with the white and yellow Cryptantha (dwarf miner's candle) and occasional fall asters and buckwheats.

FISH

Of native game fishes, the cutthroat trout and Colorado white salmon persist, though the trout are confined to a few clear spring-fed streams, notably Jones Creek and Warm Springs Creek. Powell's journal for June 21, 1869, notes that: "At night we camped at the mouth of a small creek, which affords us a good supply of trout." As Powell was then between Echo Park and Island Park, the stream was undoubtedly Jones Creek, still a favorite camping-place and fishing-stream for river travelers.

Non-native species of trout include the rainbow and German brown (Loch Leven). Neither Colorado nor Utah fish-planting records indicate that these varieties have been introduced into the area, and so it is reasonable to assume that they have migrated in high water from far up the Green in Wyoming and far up the Yampa in Colorado. Trout are almost never caught in the main rivers, which are too silty for good habitat, but undoubtedly there is some population.

Jones Creek, though a beautiful stream and highly productive of trout and the food they subsist on, is only a few miles long and not large in volume, and so could not stand up under the fishing pressure it might receive from a greatly expanded visiting public. Warm Springs Creek presents the same problem. Jones Creek can be reached by horse trail from Island Park, and adventurous sportsmen regularly get close to it with four-wheel-drive vehicles. As many as thirty-five fishermen have camped here on the opening day of the fishing season; on the other hand, Philip Hyde, photographing the Dinosaur country, camped on it for five days and never saw a mortal soul. Human beings and fishermen, like other wildlife, may be variously encountered and reported.

There are channel cat in both Green and Yampa—not native, but comprising the main catch of fishermen at the Split Mountain camp-site area, in Echo Park, and on river raft or boat trips. There are also the humpback sucker, locally called "razorback," the common sucker, carp, and chubs. Of greatest interest, however, is the Colorado River white salmon, a close relative of the Jackson Hole squaw fish and a member of the minnow family. It is reputed to attain a length of six feet and a weight of eighty pounds. The largest caught recently are around twenty pounds. It is esteemed as a food fish, having white, sweet-flavored flesh, though when the 1869 Powell expedition caught the first recorded white salmon and cooked and ate it Jack Sumner, one of the boatmen, remarked to his journal that it tasted "like a paper of pins cooked in lard oil." The numbers of Colorado River white salmon seem greatly reduced, a situation that local residents attribute to the introduction of the channel cat.

Much has been written to the effect that the reservoirs proposed for Dinosaur would provide a sportman's paradise; such published items are usually accompanied by photographs showing limit catches of large-mouthed bass taken at Lake Mead. While the proposed dams and reservoirs would eliminate little of the present sport fishing except the stream-trout-fishing in Jones Creek and Warm Springs Creek, there is small reason to believe that reservoirs in Dinosaur would provide anything comparable to what Lake Mead has produced. These would be cold waters, immensely deep, providing little fish food and few spawning-areas. Nor would the operation of huge hatcheries and the planting of large numbers of trout of catchable size do much good: an entire year's production of catchable-size trout in Colorado's twenty-five hatcheries and rearing-units would provide only half a trout for each acre-foot of water (about 300,000 gallons) in the proposed Echo Park Reservoir.

There is much more hope for fishing enthusiasts, actually, in the possibility that the Dinosaur canyons may be left as they are, for the dams planned at Flaming Gorge and at either Cross Mountain or Juniper, up the Green and the Yampa outside the Monument, would restore clear water to all the Dinosaur streams and make them a suitable habitat for large populations of game fish, as the Colorado below Hoover Dam has been transformed into trout water.

Dinosaur's wildlife habitat, none too extensive now, is closed to hunting, and consequently its unique canyon-bench-mountain ecological complex does not appreciably affect the amount of game available to the sportsman's gun, except as surplus game populations drift out of the area. It will be a better game reservoir for surrounding areas when increased recreational use brings about the end of domestic stock-grazing. It will also be a better all-round area for the recreation and inspiration of Americans when its ranges have come back and its wildlife is brought back to something like the natural balance.

We cannot bring back the dinosaurs, and most visitors will think that just as well. It is enough to imagine and to re-create them in dioramas that show them in their strange Jurassic swamps of a hundred million years ago. But it is by no means impossible to bring back most of the species that were once part of this natural unity of Dinosaur National Monument, and that have been temporarily displaced or nearly exterminated by man.

Correcting his errors, man can thrill again to the pounding wings of sandhill cranes flying up the narrow gorge of Lodore, or the thunder of bison hoofs in Island or Rainbow Park. He can have the thrill of seeing the steady silhouette of a bighorn watching his boat from the rim, or the tawny disappearing slither of a mountain lion on the Yampa cliffs. Merely the wildness, merely the beauty of natural things in their natural setting, is to most people who see it an indescribable pleasure. It is also a laboratory of science. Moreover, once we make up our minds to keep our destructive hands off, it is something that neither wears out nor changes, but can be passed on from present to future without loss.

The Ancients of the Canyons

Robert H. Lister

A SEARCH for the first traces of man in the canyons of Dinosaur would not take us back the tens of millions of years to the dinosaurs, but it would take us back a surprisingly long way. In the remote, inaccessible, and spectacular canyons of the Monument there are evidences of frequent and successive utilization of the caves, the river terraces, and even the high benches and plateau summits above the rivers during prehistoric and early historic times.

This story was not gleaned from a book or invented at a typewriter. It was literally dug out. First there were field explorations to locate living- and camping-places, called archæological sites. Out of these the best and most promising were selected, for there are many, and it is impossible for any party to excavate more than one or two or three. Then began the pick and shovel and trowel and brush work—long, dirty, hot, and hard. There is some difference between this sort of archæological excavation and that pictured in movies or described in novels. Nevertheless, it is a fascinating job, and out of the careful digging and sifting through the ruins of old houses and through the camps and trash heaps come fragments of pottery, broken tools of stone and bone, bits of basketry and sandals, the remains of food. These are the raw materials, which must be analyzed and studied and checked by the notes taken during excavation until bit by bit and detail by detail they begin to fit together and yield their little to the growing story of prehistoric Indian life in Dinosaur.

It is a story which illustrates how man finds a place to live, an environment favorable enough to let him thrive, and how he then gradually develops cultural habits that let him cope successfully with that environment. We do not yet know the complete story of Dinosaur's aboriginal peoples, and additional research will undoubtedly turn up new facts, but we do know enough to be able to outline fairly well almost three thousand years of Indian life prior to the arrival of the white man.

Prehistoric Indians found advantages in living along the Green or Yampa, whose canyons opened out into frequent small parks, valleys one to three square miles in area, where cliffs drew back from the water. In winter, when the neighboring mountains were bitter with snow and ice, the parks were mainly snow-free and several degrees warmer. The rivers and the many springs offered plenty of good water. Game, fish, and wild plant products throve in the bottoms, and along the rivers there was arable land for the few domesticated plants these people knew. Firewood came both from the bottoms and from the surrounding mountain slopes, and those same slopes, benches, and mesas provided an auxiliary supply of game and edible wild plants.

In the sandstone cliffs of Dinosaur's canyons are caves, varying in size from small shelters beneath outcropping ledges to great chambers with high arching roofs. Since the cave floors generally slope steeply downward, they are suited to human occupancy only where later deposits have accumulated on the rocky incline to form a level interior. Occasionally, prehistoric man built houses in these caves, but more generally he erected only small structures for the storage of corn and other foodstuffs. He also used caves and shelters as hideaways for a variety of perishable articles such as baskets, nets and snares, ceremonial objects, and wooden implements. Roving bands of Indians took advantage of the protection offered by these caves in bad weather.

On the canyon floors are found low terraces which grade upward from the river level several hundred feet to the foot of the cliffs. We know that the aborigines occupied these terraces from the stone artifacts, burnt rocks, and charcoal scraps they left behind them. These remains indicate camp sites that were sometimes of considerable extent, though many of the occupational areas have unfortunately been destroyed by the high spring water which has cut up the terraces.

At the top of the cliffs, among the cedar breaks on the broad benches and isolated mesas, aboriginal sites are many and large. Characteristically they are located on spurs of land between deeply eroded gullies. Fire hearths and burnt stones are exposed at the surface, along with great quantities of chipped-stone implements and flakes, and occasional metates and manos for grinding corn and seeds. Fallen poles and timbers in the vicinity of the ancient hearth areas are most likely the leftovers from tipis or wickiups of much more recent historic Indians, probably Utes.

The mountain summits, which frequently here take the form of wide tablelands, likewise abound in archæological sites. They are marked almost exclusively by surface finds of stone artifacts, and the number of places littered with flakes and spalls suggests a widespread occupation of the mountains. Sites on Douglas Mountain and Blue Mountain have exposures of vertical stone slabs, indicating the presence of slab-lined storage pits like those found in the caves.

But perhaps the most conspicuous aboriginal remains in Dinosaur are the cliff murals. They consist of painted murals (pictographs), usually executed in red ocher, and carved murals (petroglyphs) pecked upon the face of the cliff with a sharp stone. The carved or pecked figures are usually well preserved, although dimmed somewhat by the disintegration of the rock surface.

Whatever the cliff decorations may have meant to the Indian artist, for us they have little symbolic or narrative significance. We cannot read them: the Indians did not use their art to inform us. We can recognize humans, animals, footprints, weapons, and other objects, but apparently the murals do not represent an attempt at writing.

A few murals are historic. Historic Indians, probably Utes, depicted the horse in some of their murals near Monument Headquarters, and there is a multi-masted sailing-vessel that old-timer Pat Lynch pecked into the middle of a prehistoric panel in Castle Park. However, the great majority are certainly prehistoric, and the square-shouldered human beings, the animals, the squash-blossom coiffure, the footprints, the bow and arrow, and the great horned human figures ornamented with necklaces are all forms that relate these cliff pictures to those found in neighboring archæological areas. In Rainbow Park, for instance, there is a painting of the hunch-backed flute-player who is known among the Hopi Indians of Arizona as Kokopeli, and whose picture is widespread in the area of the prehistoric Pueblos, both on painted pottery and in cliff murals.

From among the wealth of sites offered by Dinosaur, several expeditions have taken a sampling. Some such investigations were undertaken as sidelights of river-running expeditions or mountaineering ventures, but in recent years several individuals as well as scientific parties sponsored by institutions have made trips into Dinosaur for the express purpose of recording archæological remains. Among organizations that have put expeditions in the field are the Colorado State Historical Society, the National Park Service, and the University of Colorado.

Between 1939 and 1949 the University of Colorado had several parties conducting intensive excavations in Castle Park, on the Yampa. That area was chosen not only because it offered several kinds of sites, but because Mr. and Mrs. Charley Mantle, the owners of the ranch in Castle Park, were well versed in the antiquities of the region and helped out the field activities in many ways. Actually, the detailed knowledge of prehistoric Indian cultures in Dinosaur comes primarily from the three excavations conducted in Castle Park; general surveys, though they provide evidence about types of Indian remains and their distribution and prevalence, do not turn up the careful and detailed information: to get that, you have to dig.

The first site to be studied was Mantle's Cave, a large vaulted chamber over 350 feet long and 130 feet from front to rear, located at the head of a short box canyon. Rocks from the roof of the cave and from the cliff above it have lodged on the slope in front, forming an anchorage for alluvium and wind-blown dirt, so that a high talus cone has been built up at the mouth of the cave. Behind the talus cone there is an extensive rockfall where part of the roof has collapsed. It seems to have occurred while the cave was occupied. Between the rockfall and the back wall of the cave there is a relatively level floor.

On top of the rockfall of massive sandstone blocks buried in silt and sand the prehistoric Indians built masonry granaries which are the most noticeable cultural remains in the cave. At several places around the cave floor they dug storage pits, some of them lined with stone, slabs. Both granaries and pits must have been used principally for storing food, but the contents were removed in ancient times. All that they yielded to the careful diggers was shreds of cedar bark, occasional artifacts, trash, and remnants of corn. Covers for these storage granaries and pits were of several kinds. Some apparently were of mud daubed over a horizontal framework of sticks. Others were flat stones or inverted baskets.

To unearth the story that this cave had to tell, the University of Colorado party dug a number of deep test trenches in the area of the rockfall and in the cave floor, the principal purpose being to determine the nature of the cave deposits and the depth of cultural remains. In several places, poorly defined occupational levels were detected—hard-packed surfaces, but not plastered and not burned, evidently produced by casual traffic on the littered natural surface of the cave. If Mantle's Cave had been regularly used as a residence, those occupational levels would have been, in all probability, much better defined.

Over most of the cave floor the levels were irregular and the cultural debris considerably mixed, for several reasons. Aboriginal digging of storage pits stirred up and mingled the layers of the cave; artifacts lost or hidden in cracks and crevices were covered over; centuries of wind and water deposited sand and silt unequally on the floor; and rodents dug things up and scratched them to the surface and covered them again. As a result, locating and dating the different finds was made more difficult.

Few of the archæological specimens found in Mantle's Cave were associated with structures. Instead, they were shallowly buried in the sand, on or above the occupational levels marked by scattered cedar bark, animal bones, and other refuse. It seems certain that many of these objects were left lying on the surface and were later covered by wind-blown sand, and that others were hidden in shallow holes or pockets or cracks, and forgotten.

Six caches of artifacts were recovered from Mantle's Cave, some by the several University of Colorado expeditions and others earlier. All are now in the University of Colorado Museum. Of the six caches, three are important, and one is unique. This is a buckskin pouch found in a shallow pit dug into the cave floor. It contained among other things a headdress of feathers and ermine—the only one, to our knowledge, ever found in an archæological site. Almost perfectly preserved, it is the finest specimen in the Castle Park collection. The headband is made from over 350 black and orange feathers from the flicker, a type of woodpecker; it probably used up more than sixty flickers. Along the lower front edge of the band there is a trimming of ermine, made from the skins of three winter weasels. Along the back edge is a buckskin backing strip the same width as the ermine band, and the feathers are held in place between the two strips by lacings of fiber. Near either end of the band are fastened the buckskin thongs that tied around the head and held the headdress in place. The similarity of this apparently ancient ceremonial headdress to flicker-feather headbands of historic California Indians is remarkable, but the cultural connections, if any, are still obscure.

Another cache in Mantle's Cave contained a headdress made from the tanned scalp of a deer, presumably a doe, with the ears attached and ribbed with heavy feather quills to make them stand erect. Associated with this find was a pair of deerskin moccasins.

Another cache, a basket containing several fishhooks and many snares for small animals, was evidently buried in the sandy floor of the cave by an ancient hunter who for some reason never returned to retrieve his possessions. They would have been wealth to a hunter: the fishhooks were made by tying a bone barb to a curved wooden shaft. The game snares were of tapered fiber cordage, with nooses at the ends. Some examples had a wooden tube which perhaps was employed as a keeper for the noose.

Beyond those three notable caches, Mantle's Cave produced a variety of chipped-stone implements including knives, scrapers, drills, and arrow and spear points, as well as metates and manos. The dryness of the cave has permitted the preservation of a number of items made of perishable materials such as plant fibers, wood, and leather. These Indians obviously made baskets, matting, twined bags, and cordage from a variety of fibers. They used wood for arrow and spear shafts, knife handles, and an implement used in harvesting seeds. They made bags, pouches, and moccasins of leather, generally deerskin, and cut or polished awls, scrapers, tubes, and gaming-pieces from mammal bones. A few scraps of cloth made from fur and feathers indicate that they wove warm blankets of such materials. Only broken pottery was found in Mantle's Cave. The ware is culinary, plain gray and probably round-bottomed; most of the fragments were found covered with scales of ash and carbon.

Petroglyphs at McKee Spring.

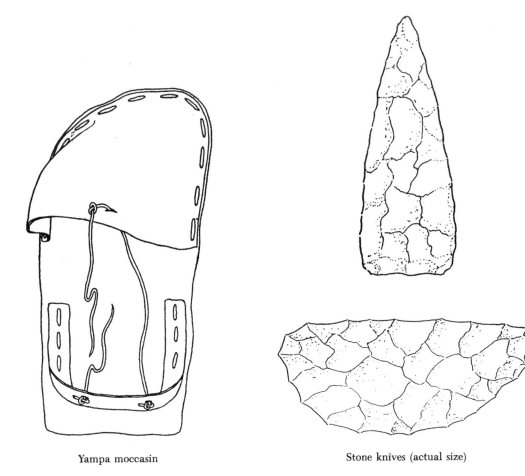

Yampa moccasin

Stone knives (actual size)

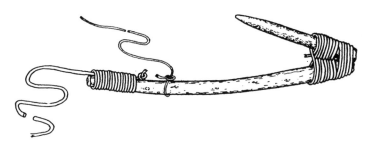

Fishhook of bone and wood

What did these prehistoric Indians eat? Remains of foodstuffs found in Mantle's Cave point to an economy based on hunting and gathering as well as agriculture. The burnt and broken bones of deer, cottontail rabbits, prairie dogs, and fish tell us something. So do the grass seeds and root fragments sifted out of the trash in the bottoms of storage pits. Probably berries, pine nuts, and the fruits of cactus were gathered and eaten, and even in prehistoric times three plants were cultivated: corn, squash, and pumpkins.

The age of the Mantle's Cave remains can be estimated by comparing certain items found in the cave with similar objects present in neighboring areas where fairly accurate chronologies have been established. Dinosaur lies at the northern edge of the prehistoric Pueblo Indian culture area, where extensive excavations have worked out the stages of culture growth in considerable detail. In the Pueblo area it is known that certain types of baskets, pottery, stone and bone implements, and other cultural manifestations are characteristic of particular time periods. The Mantle's Cave finds are closely related to the Fremont Culture, a phase of Pueblo development which centered in east-central Utah and flourished between A.D. 400 and 800. Mantle's Cave thus takes us back a maximum of about fifteen hundred years.

Marigold Cave, a large vault situated high above the Yampa at the lower end of Castle Park, adds to the evidence. Excavation in the two long narrow ledges which show signs of human habitation revealed several slab-lined storage pits and what appeared to be a cooking-pit. Numerous artifacts of stone, bone, clay, and vegetable fibers were similar to specimens recovered in Mantle's Cave. Particularly interesting was an assortment of small clay figurines in the shapes of birds.

Here there were shelters, which were constructed quite uniformly by setting two posts in the ground, joining them across the tops with a horizontal beam, and laying on a lean-to roof of reeds and cedar bark held in place by thin sandstone slabs. The front side was open, the floor was mud-plastered and contained fire pits and in some cases storage pits.

The artifacts from Marigold Cave indicate that it was occupied during the last phase of the Fremont Culture. A post used in one of the shelters was dated by the tree-ring method and was estimated to have been cut between A.D. 700 and 800, a date which is entirely in harmony with the archæological evidence.

The third excavation made in Castle Park carries us back to an altogether different, and much older, cultural horizon. It was made at Hell's Midden, a large stratified refuse deposit—which in less polite terms means an ancient dumpground. Under a rock ledge that had been used as a shelter through many centuries, trash and litter and junk and lost objects built up to a thickness of many feet. The job of excavation was not spectacular. It consisted merely of digging a wide trench clear through the midden and down to the bottom of all cultural deposits. Since this junk accumulated in an exposed site, few things made of perishable materials lasted. But more durable artifacts were found all the way down to a depth of fifteen feet. The upper layers contained Fremont Culture items similar to those of Mantle's and Marigold caves. But the middle and lower sections contained stone and bone tools from a much earlier occupation.

The Indians of the Fremont Culture were at least part-time farmers; those whose relics show up in the lower layers of Hell's Midden lived entirely by hunting and gathering. They ate deer, mountain sheep, bison, fox, beaver, prairie dog, marmot, rabbit, wood rat, fish—and threw their gnawed bones on the trash heap below the shelf. They had, apparently, neither pottery nor corn, but they made stone projectile points, knives, and scrapers, as well as a few grinding-implements. Some of these are similar to types found in the Mojave Desert of California.

At several points in Hell's Midden, excavation revealed fire hearths, storage pits, and other evidence of occupation levels, but there was nothing to suggest that houses or shelters were built under the overhanging ledge. The ledge sheltered them, the floor held their hearths and received their trash and was packed hard by their feet. Gradually the trash built up, so that new occupational levels were established on top of the old. The strata of the midden suggest that occupation was periodic rather than continuous, for there is a rather clear-cut alternation of cultural debris—charcoal, ash, artifacts, and hard-packed dirt—with "natural" levels of water-laid or wind-laid sand and silt.

The upper levels of Hell's Midden reveal a culture contemporaneous and identical with that of Mantle's and Marigold caves—somewhere between A.D. 400 and 800. But the earlier hunting and gathering stages may go back in time as far as 1500 B.C., a good two thousand years earlier. This estimate is based on the depth of the material in the midden and on the similarities of some of the projectile points with those found in the Mojave Desert.

From that very old hunting and gathering culture to the end of the Fremont Culture, the story is reasonably clear. What happened at the end of Fremont times is not so clear. We simply do not know whether for some reason the Fremont people left, or whether there was a continuous but as yet unstudied occupation from A.D. 800 until early historic times, when we know Indians of the Ute tribe were living in the area. Excavation of more cave sites and some of the open sites on terraces, mesas, and mountain summits may supply the answer. It is possible that Athapascan-speaking tribes who wandered into the Southwest from the north and became the ancestors of the Apache and Navajo passed through Dinosaur. Some of the camp sites may be attributed to these people; others, especially those where tipi or wickiup remains can be seen, are more probably the fairly recent leavings of the Utes.

The archæological relics of Dinosaur National Monument are extensive, though not spectacular. They tell a story of a hunting and fishing and gathering culture possibly as old as 1500 B.C., which gradually turned to a more settled existence in the canyons after the people learned to cultivate corn about A.D. 400. From then on for several centuries they lived a settled and probably peaceful existence in the canyons, building houses of poles, matting, and hides along the river, and using the caves for occasional shelter and for the storage and hiding of food and valuables. We have neither skeletons nor traditions to tell us anything about their physical and racial and tribal identities, and the murals which at first glance look like their most eloquent memorial seem to mean little.

The agricultural horizon of the Dinosaur people is virtually identical with that of the Fremont Culture immediately to the southeast. Fremont Culture was essentially Pueblo in content, but it seems to have been lazy or isolated, and it was little stimulated by the appearance now and then of new arts such as pottery-making, pueblo-building, and the cultivation of beans, all of which flourished farther south in the nuclear Pueblo area. For reasons that we can only guess at as we guess at the causes of the cultural dead end around A.D. 800, the Dinosaur Indians remained laggards, unchallenged and unresponsive in their remote and beautiful backwater. Perhaps, living where they did, they were altogether too contented.

Fast Water

Otis "Dock" Marston

FROM THE DAYS of the rash and reckless mountain men (most of whom shunned the fast water even though the rivers offered them a highway to the harvest of furs they craved) the canyons of Dinosaur have had a reputation far worse than they deserved. Anyone who goes boating on them now goes with ninety years of experience behind him. He can go safely and fast, in properly designed boats, and he runs many rapids that in the past were cautiously lined or even portaged. He goes, generally, for fun, and the risk involved is so small that it does not warrant any increase in life-insurance rates. With good boats and good boatmen, these canyons are considerably less dangerous than the traffic of any American highway.

The change by which a fearsome river has become a playground has involved two things: the dissipation of wild tales and bogey stories about Niagaras, "sucks," and cataracts on the one hand; and the development of suitable boats and techniques on the other. The second is actually the more important, for good boats proved at once that the river was far less terrible than it had been cracked up to be. In bad boats the Green was toilsome and sometimes dangerous. In good boats, well handled, the Green and its milder sister the Yampa are merely exhilarating.

Actually, almost every sort of boat has started down the Green, and many sorts have made it through the Dinosaur canyons. General Ashley, who first challenged the trappers' superstitious fears of the river in 1825, went all the way down to the mouth of the Uinta or Duchesne River, in bullboats—and a bullboat was nothing but a pole frame thirty feet long, with twelve feet of beam, covered with pitch-smeared buffalo skins. Below the "Tewinty" Ashley went on in a wooden canoe with three of the men for another twenty to fifty miles before starting back overland. Ashley's journal admits sixteen portages, most of them in Lodore, which involved the utmost difficulty and labor. There are not sixteen places in that stretch of river that are serious navigational hazards, and we must conclude that the bullboat, though it did provide transport, was hardly adequate for handling fast water.

Ashley's report, if it had been made public early, would have been a report less of danger than of toilsome labor. Unfortunately the report that did become public was that of Ashley's mulatto wrangler James P. Beckwourth,[1] who cooked up a yarn about rescuing his commander from the Green River Suck. This was the maw of a mad river descending two hundred feet in a distance of six to eight miles, and lavishly propertied with rocks, ledges, sharp curves, perpendicular cliffs, eddies, starvation, and inevitable death. Some of Beckwourth's imaginary horrors clung to the river for a long time, and are dragged out even today when someone wants to represent these canyons as too dangerous for ordinary mortals.

During the period of the fur-traders there must certainly have been other penetrations of the Dinosaur canyons besides Ashley's. Denis Julien, trapping out of Fort Robidoux in the Uinta Valley, left his name on the cliff walls of the lower Green and Cataract Canyon, and near the inscription in Hell Roaring Canyon, in addition to his name and the date 1836, there is the crude drawing of a boat. Julien's river paths remain obscure, but it could well be that he also boated on the upper Green in what is now Dinosaur.

There were traders in Brown's Hole (now Brown's Park) from the 1820's on, and in 1836 or 1837 Philip Thompson, William Craig, and a man named St. Clair or Sinclair built a fort there, naming it Fort Davy Crockett. They displaced Baptiste and Bibleback Brown, who had arrived some years earlier. Spanish traders frequented the Hole between 1800 and 1850, but what

---

1 In *The Life and Adventures of James P. Beckwourth* (New York: Harper & Bros.; 1856).

experience they may have had on the river is unknown. Thomas J. Farnham tells of two Catholic missionaries and their servant who disappeared, and of a party of trappers who thrust their battered boat ashore and succeeded in leaping upon the crags. But those expeditions are a part of legend, uncorroborated and dubious; and though Joseph L. Meek descended through the Green River canyons from Brown's Park to the mouth of the Uinta in December 1839, he did it on horseback, aided by the ice, and not by boat.

William Lewis Manly's group made the second recorded descent, in 1849. They started in a sunken and rehabilitated ferry twelve feet long and six or seven wide, and the crude hulk got them, with much labor working it off rocks, as far as Red Canyon. They lined Ashley Falls, but three hundred yards downriver, while attempting another lining, they put the scow on a rock and couldn't budge it. A substitute was chopped out of pine trees—two canoes fifteen feet long and two wide, lashed together for stability. Those wouldn't carry the load; they made another one twenty-five feet long.

Even those crude dugouts got them through the canyons, though with enormous labor. At one point, probably in Lodore, they found abandoned equipment and a note pasted on a tree indicating that some previous party had left the river in favor of a land route to Salt Lake. The Manly party stuck to their dugouts clear through the Uinta Valley, capsized both small canoes in either Desolation or Gray Canyon, and eventually, near the present town of Greenriver, Utah, followed the example of their unknown predecessors and went overland to Salt Lake.

The first boats specifically designed for the river were those of Major Powell's expedition in 1869, and they were designed badly. Three were oak-planked and double-ribbed, made for carrying freight, and had decked compartments fore and aft. Each was manned by two oarsmen. The pine-planked boat was sixteen feet long and driven by four oars. It had the special feature of a sharp cutwater, which the designers mistakenly thought would make for fast rowing.

Heavily overloaded and with inexperienced boatmen, the Powell party reaped a harvest of unnecessary mishaps and adventures, and after a succession of collisions, linings, portages, spinning whirlpools, soakings of dunnage and supplies, fire in camp, and the loss of one boat in the rapid they named Disaster Falls, they got out into the Uinta Valley on June 26, a little more than a month after they had left Green River, Wyoming. A significant part of the mileage had been overland, and one of the basic scientific facts established had been that most of the rapids had shores adequate for lining and portaging.

On that first trip, despite the clumsiness of his boats, Powell made it, minus four of his original party, down to the mouth of the Virgin, in Nevada, completing the first traverse of the Grand Canyon. In May 1871, with an appropriation from Congress to assist him, he set off for a second run. His three boats were as brutally overloaded as his first ones had been, and the design was not much better. They were twenty-two feet long, with five feet of beam. The hull design remained the same: round-bottomed, pointed fore and aft. The one improvement was the addition of a four-foot covered compartment amidships to aid in flotation. Of the men, only Powell had any rough-water experience. On the mid-cabin of the *Emma Dean*, the pilot boat, was bolted an armchair, from which Powell scouted the river ahead. There has seldom been anything so absurd on the river.

Their experiences, first publicized through Frederick S. Dellenbaugh's *A Canyon Voyage* in 1908, were similar to those of the first party: swampings in upper Red Canyon, lining of Ashley Falls. Lodore's twenty miles took them nine days of portages, linings, capsizings, and founderings. They tried to row up the canyon of the Yampa in the *Emma Dean* and gained only about eleven miles in four days. Near the Yampa's mouth, two of the party thought they found a dangerous whirlpool perilously like Beckwourth's Suck. Through Split Mountain Canyon they lined four of the six and seven-eighths miles: in 1952 a skiff cruised this canyon in thirty-two minutes—a perfect illustration of the difference a little good design makes.

The bad design and overloading of Powell's boats is indicated also by the fact that between Green River and the mouth of Split Mountain neither of his expeditions piloted their boats through fast water of any consequence, though every rapid in this section has been run numerous times since. Major Powell was an able geologist, ethnologist, politician, and philosopher, but he was not the most skilled boating leader the river has seen, by quite a long way. Neither he nor Dellenbaugh ever did learn the lessons of fast-water equipment, and both he and Dellenbaugh were advocating the 1871–2 design until their deaths. Their experience with that design, written up in Powell's report and in Dellenbaugh's books, helped to perpetuate the myth of the fearsome rivers.

Still, the tales that went around about the canyons did not prevent others from taking a chance, sometimes successfully, sometimes not. About 1891 two Snyders, father and son, from Vernal, Utah, came to grief in Lodore and borrowed horses to ride out. But 1896 produced one of the truly significant advances in river travel.

On the river's bank at Green River, George F. Flavell and Ramon Montos made their own boat, a fifteen-and-a-half-footer with a five-foot beam. Flavell knew rough water, and built accordingly: his boat was flat-bottomed, with a high tapered bow, broad stern, and no compartments. He and Montos ran in August, on low water, but their light boat bounced easily through twenty riffles in Flaming Gorge within two hours, and they ran all the rapids in Red Canyon, including Ashley Falls, with minimum difficulty. Those rapids, though not by any means the roughest in the upper stretch of river, had made trouble for Ashley, grounded Manly's barge, and caused endless labor to Powell's crews. The light skiff ran them with comparative ease.

In Brown's Park, old-timers gave Flavell the fearful-myth treatment, but when he found that none of them had ever personally been in the canyons he went ahead. He was impressed enough to line four of Lodore's rapids—the little one above Disaster Falls, Upper and Lower Disaster Falls, and Hell's Half Mile. The rest of them he and Montos ran, and except for a rock they hit in Split Mountain they experienced none of the toils and dangers that previous parties had met. Skill and adequate equipment took them all the way through the canyons, including the Grand Canyon, to Needles, and they lined only twice more—in Cataract Canyon and at Soap Creek in Marble Canyon.

Flavell's success with light flat-bottomed craft set the stage for one of the greatest outdoorsmen and boatmen of them all, Nathaniel Galloway.

Galloway lived at Vernal, where for twelve years prior to 1896 he had made a living as a trapper and prospector. Five times, by that year, he had been through the canyons of the upper Green, once taking his thirteen-year-old son John along. He had evolved a light, mobile, flat-bottomed boat, and had developed or introduced the technique of going stern-first through rough water. He was not after publicity, or even adventure; he was after what he called "simple pursuits"—furs and signs of color in the gravel.

In September 1896 he dropped his boat in the water at Henry's Fork, at the northern edge of the Uintas, and with his young son Than ran down through Flaming Gorge, Kingfisher, and Red canyons—"smooth sailing to a man accustomed to navigate rough water." In Little Hole, below Ashley Falls, he came upon two prospectors, William Chesley Richmond and Frank Leland, who had built a boat and a placer mining outfit and had set out a few days before from Henry's Fork, towing the mining-equipment behind them. They were overloaded, and when they found an old boat buried in the sand they loaded the mining-equipment on it. At Ashley Falls Richmond tried a dash with the old boat: that took care of the boat, the overload, and everything else. When the Galloways joined them and proposed a run clear through the Grand Canyon, Richmond was game. Leland went out by land.

Neither boat had compartments. Using the stern-first technique through rapids, they ran everything in Lodore but Lower Disaster Falls, which they lined, and Hell's Half Mile, which they portaged. The rest of the run to Alhandra Ferry lacked sufficient adventure to warrant comment. For the lower part of the trip they changed to two Galloway boats that had been cached near the head of Desolation Canyon, and that were fitted with canvas decking fore and aft. The trip ended without mishap at Needles in February 1897.

The next year, when Galloway was working for Robert Brewster Stanton in Glen Canyon on the Colorado, Julius F. Stone, a Columbus, Ohio, millionaire, came to the river to inspect placer operations, and jaunted with Galloway through Glen Canyon to Lees Ferry. The canyon bug bit him: he was led to Powell's report, and from the report to Powell himself. In that interview Stone thought Powell put him off, and he determined to run the river himself, checking on Powell as he went. When he finally did so, eleven years later, he brought Galloway east to supervise the building of his boats.

In 1898, in his routine work, Galloway cruised from Green River, Wyoming, to Greenriver, Utah, and in April and May 1909 he and his son Parley made the traverse of the Yampa and down through Whirlpool and Split Mountain canyons on the flood. Between 1903 and this Yampa

Running a rapid, nineteenth-century style, with the Powell Expedition of 1869.

Artist and assistant topographer Frederick Samuel Dellenbaugh sits by the Green River in Lodore Canyon during Powell's second expedition in 1871.

run, Parley had already had four trips in the upper Green River canyons. Studying the superlatives in Dellenbaugh's *A Canyon Voyage*, the Galloways wished they could invite the author along so he could run the river instead of walking it.

The boats that Galloway built for Stone were sixteen and a half feet long, with four feet of beam. Rake fore and aft from center was ten inches. Solid bulkheads divided the hull into two three-foot compartments in the bow, a five-foot cockpit, and a three-foot and a two-and-a- half-foot compartment aft. Two compartments were decked and two had canvas covers, and in rapids canvas fenders eighteen inches high were rigged around the cockpits. The weight of the unloaded boat was 243 pounds. The revolutionary

Flat-bottomed neoprene rafts provide a much safer journey down the rivers of Dinosaur National Monument than the pine-planked boats used a century ago. Here a few of these rafts drift along the Yampa toward Tiger Wall.

concept in Galloway's design was to provide a unit light enough to stay clear of rocks. Powell had attempted construction stronger than the rocks.

Lightness proved out for Stone. Leaving Green River on September 12, 1909, on low water, the party of five ran everything down to Brown's Park, including Ashley Falls. In Lodore they unloaded the boats and each was run through Upper and Lower Disaster Falls by Galloway. Only Hell's Half Mile was portaged. All the boats ran all the rapids in Whirlpool and Split Mountain canyons, although Galloway took them one by one through Moonshine Draw. Charles Sharp, one of the boatmen, foundered in Desolation Canyon, and Seymour Dubendorff, the other boatman, capsized in Cataract Canyon and again in Grand Canyon, where he left his name on a rapid. But these were mere upsets; only twenty-one linings and seven portages were logged for the whole canyon trip, and the excellent condition of the boats at the end proved the soundness of their design.

The photographic voyage of the brothers Ellsworth and Emory Kolb in 1911 was made in slightly heavier boats built from the Stone-Galloway plans. Neither the Kolbs nor James Fagin, who started with them, could row, a fact which insured adventure. Linings and portages alternated with founderings through Lodore, and Fagin allowed at Echo Park that he had seen the elephant and would retire. But the Kolbs ran Whirlpool and Split Mountain without lining, and they went on to finish the traverse of the Grand Canyon, picking up a helper named Hubert Lauzon at Bright Angel Creek en route. From the time light and maneuverable flat-bottomed boats began to be used on the rivers, the rapids began to look less and less terrifying.

The Kolb brothers were closely followed from Green River, Wyoming, to Greenriver, Utah, by John Galloway. A month later Nat Galloway traveled the same course, which by this time was for him practically a milk run.

The United States Geological Survey, when it surveyed the upper Green River canyons in 1922, adopted the Stone-Galloway type of boat, using craft that had been built by the Utah Power and Light Company for its survey of Flaming Gorge. Length had been increased to eighteen feet, but the beam remained at four feet.

The boats left Green River on July 13, 1922, and had no trouble with Red Canyon, but did have trouble with rocks above Upper Disaster Falls. The party did not recognize the infamous rapid itself. Lower Disaster was portaged, and at Hell's Half Mile they nosed the empty boats through the middle section. Nosing, called a "kick portage" by the second Powell crew, involves walking along the edge of the river and working the boat down. Whirlpool and Split Mountain canyons were run freely. The principal boatman on that trip was Bert Loper, who died of a heart attack twenty-seven years later while running Marble Canyon on the Colorado. He was then two weeks short of eighty years old.

In the spring of 1926 John Galloway ran the canyons again, trapping from Green River in Wyoming to Ouray in Utah.

By that time the river trip was not an exploration or even an expedition, but an excursion, and people were as likely to experiment to find the most dangerous and daring boat design as they once had been to find the best and safest.

The first tourist excursion was the Todd-Page party of 1926—three Princeton men, a boatman, and a cook. They used two of the Geological Survey boats from 1922. Ashley Falls was run with full loads and passengers; the crew put on life-preservers and swam through for the hell of it. One boat foundered in Red Canyon Rapid, but was freed with a Spanish windlass. The other was nosed around this rapid, and both were nosed around Upper and Lower Disaster Falls. Elwyn Blake, the boatman, hung a boat on a rock trying to run Hell's Half Mile, and one of the Princeton graduates, F. Lemoyne Page, hit a rock but got through with the other. Between Rippling Brook and the mouth of the Yampa one boat was pinned on a boulder and lost, and they finished in the other, some of the crew walking around rapids but the boat running them all.

Still, not every party was so competent or so lucky or so well prepared. A party sponsored by the *Denver Post* had a couple of lively weeks on the Yampa from August 19 to September 4, 1928. The leader was A. G. Birch; the party included Bert Moritz, Fred Dunham, and photographer Charles E. Mace. Their two boats, sixteen and a half feet long, with four and a half feet of beam, were named the *Leakin Lena* and the *Prickly Heat*. Their wild and strenuous adventures reached a peak when one boat was torn to pieces in the rocks, and near Castle Park they abandoned the other boat and the expedition.

Boat experiments, or inexperience, accounted for three out of four deaths, all on the Yampa, in 1929. John Powers, of Youghall, Colorado, disappeared when his homemade boat was wrecked. In July two youths from Chicago attempting a traverse of the canyon in a canvas collapsible boat remained unreported. In September a man named Brown, from Wyoming, was lost below Lily Park.

On September 10, 1932, Fred Launer, a Salt Lake furrier, assembled a sixteen-foot Berger foldboat at Green River, loaded aboard aging Dr. Charles G. Plummer and a good supply of raisins and peanuts, and pushed off. Dr. Plummer walked around all the rough water and made an extensive photographic record. The fabric of the collapsible craft was twice punctured, but otherwise the foldboat completed its first passage without mishap.

The river continued to lure local boys and men into adventure. A year before the first foldboat run, Bus Hatch, now the daddy of Green River and Yampa boatmen, made his first try at the canyons with Frank Swain, C. L. Hatch, and Royce Mowrey. Their open skiff, which they had run bow-first instead of following Galloway's stern-first technique in rough water, arrived battered and leaky in Jensen after four days. They had cap-sized in Lodore and lost most of their provisions, but the canyon fever had them. Next year they were back with new boats, one of which they abandoned in Lodore.

Two years later the Hatch-Swain crew ran the Grand Canyon with a fleet that included one experimental boat made of marine plywood—ever since that time a common material in river craft. Bus Hatch has led one other Grand Canyon expedition, in 1954, but by and large he and his com-panions have stuck to the upper river, the Dinosaur country. Most of their multiplying trips in recent years have been floated in neoprene rafts. These, clumsy but relatively safe, have turned out to be nearly foolproof for large parties, especially those containing women, children, the lame, the halt, and the blind. Everybody runs the river now.

And adventurous experiment has not ceased. In 1936 Tony Backus started through alone in a scow-type, partially decked punt: he pulled it up on the talus of the first rapid in Lodore and tried it no farther. But on October 4 of the next year Haldane "Buzz" Holmstrom started alone from Green River in his beautifully built sixteen-foot boat constructed on the Galloway-Stone pattern. Weight approached five hundred pounds. Holmstrom ran Ashley Falls and portaged Red Canyon Rapid. At Upper Disaster Falls he portaged his dunnage; Lower Disaster and Triplet he lined. In Hell's Half Mile, fortunate skids off two rocks let his unloaded boat through. Whirlpool and Split Mountain provided tricky rock slaloms in the low water, but no portaging or lining was required. Holmstrom completed his trip to Hoover Dam for the first and only solo traverse of the Grand Canyon. He would not have been likely to do it in any other kind of boat.

In 1938 Holmstrom went down a second time, leading an expedition promoted by Amos Burg and partially financed by Julius Stone. The pur-pose was photography, but the feature of the trip was the experimental boat used by Burg—an inflated rubber boat sixteen feet long, with a beam of five and a half feet, and weighing only eighty-three pounds. That was the first inflated rubber equipment on the river, the forerunner of the neoprene rafts.

It was one hundred and thirteen years after Ashley's first running of the canyons before the first woman tried it. She was a Paris import, Geneviève de Colmont, who with Bernard de Colmont and Antoine de Seynes pulled out from Green River in three folding kayaks on September 13, 1938. The kayaks were sixteen feet long, with a two-foot- eight-inch beam. Their principal load was canned beer; the French sportsmen seemed to fear bad drinking-water more than bad running water. It was appropriate, since she was to have the honor of being the first through Dinosaur's canyons, that the lady was beautiful. De Colmont cracked up in Hell's Half Mile, but she and de Seynes made it through. They all left the river at Lees Ferry without attempting Marble or Grand canyons.

By that time river traffic was getting heavy. You couldn't depend on solitude any more, even in the most remote canyons. The French trio met a five-man party in Little Hole, using two boats built to the specifications of Bus Hatch, and a few days after the Frenchmen and this Rasmussen-de Spain-Eddington-Kay-Clyde party had floated out into the open at Jensen, twenty-three-year-old Stewart Gardiner shot through Lodore, Whirlpool, and Split Mountain in six days in a folding kayak. The next year Gardiner did it again with a companion named Alexander "Zee" Grant, and the year after that, Grant made the first kayak run through the Grand Canyon.

1939 was also the year in which Charles Fulton Mann repeated the course of the Frenchmen from Green River to Lees Ferry. His kayak was only fourteen feet long, and weighed thirty-five pounds. Red Canyon tore eight holes in his hull fabric, Lower Disaster capsized him. After three more capsizings en route, he made it to Lees Ferry with a badly smashed boat and little food. He had lined two rapids and portaged two others, and his trip, along with those of the Frenchmen, Gardiner, and Grant, had demonstrated that kayaks in skilled hands could get you through the can-yons—if you wanted adventure and didn't care about comfort and were not too particular about safety.

By June 1940, when Bert Loper and Laphene (Don) Harris came down the river trailing the first Green-Colorado expedition of Norman Nevills, river excursions had come to be so common they hardly warranted attention or counting. Loper in 1940 was seventy years old: he handled his own skiff. In the three sadiron-shaped plywood skiffs of the Nevills party were Nevills's wife, Doris, and another woman, Mildred Baker. On June 27 the party ran into Buzz Holmstrom and camped with him. The canyons were getting to be places where you held family picnics and accidentally encountered old friends.

The tourist business, which was held down by the war, expanded immediately after it, and the people who have run one or another section of the Yampa, Green, and Colorado canyons now number several thousand. They will soon reach several thousand every month, in season.

On any well-organized river trip there is fun (and a kind that can't be had in any other way) with a minimum of strain. Lack of organization wrecked more early river-runners than rocks or waves did. Reasonable safety demands adequate equipment, supplies, and skill. Lack of any one of these is virtual insurance that trials and adventures will be encountered.

For increasing thousands, nevertheless, the rapids are the most fascinating thing in Dinosaur, providing a sport that is relatively inexpensive, that is as exciting as skiing, and that can be enjoyed by the whole family in company. A trip down through the canyons adds the thrills of fast water to the beauty of cliff colors and rock sculpture, the lovely water-muttering quiet of a camp in one of the "holes," the constant interest of wildlife, caves, prehistoric murals. But the pleasures of river-running may not last: the dams proposed for Echo Park and Split Mountain would do more than drown the parks and the camping-places, obliterate the murals, foreshorten the cliffs, and wipe out the archæological sites. They would also eliminate every rapid on both Yampa and Green, from Lily Park and Brown's Park to the mouth of Split Mountain. In their place would be a long still-water reservoir with mud banks.

But the fast water is still there in 1955, and there are competent guides and boats available at several points. Deans of the upper-river guides are Bus Hatch, of Vernal, Utah, and Don Harris, President of the Western River Guides Association, of Salt Lake City. A. K. Reynolds, of Green River, Wyoming, is equipped to provide all reasonable safety on the upper Green.

One thing these men cannot do is provide immunity to the fever that takes all rapids-runners. For that disease there is no immunity except to avoid all sources, even pictorial sources, of contagion. There is absolutely no cure. The only alleviation—and a temporary one at that—is to run the rapids again.

A Short Look at Eden

David Bradley

ONE THING YOU DISCOVER about Dinosaur National Monument, when you have approached and entered it from several directions, is its near-perfect unity. At most other national parks and monuments you look beyond the borders and see land that should be inside but isn't, or you look inside and see country that shouldn't be part of that precious "fraction of one per cent" but is. You wonder why Yosemite Park fails to extend its wilderness-protection to Shadow Lake and the Minarets, and why the boundary of Olympic National Park is a zigzag of partly surveyed section lines that ignore the natural features.

Dinosaur raises no such questions. It is nearly whole, nearly self-contained, with its natural (and magnificent) water gateways and few arbitrary breaks in its logical boundaries. If the south side were straightened up by filling in the vulnerable gap between Round Top and Doc's Valley, and some acreage were added east of the Canyon of Lodore, the preserve would be as ideally outlined as section-line bounds can make it.

The unity which is perceived gradually through exploration of the Monument's roads and rivers is apparent at once from the air. From up there the slightly domed plateau known as Blue Mountain is not a plateau at all, but a gathering of hills and sharp ridges and benches and chasms, stained in its intaglio depths with the colors of the rock's heart, but all of it washed and splotched with blue—the blue of ponderosa pine and Douglas fir, of sage and juniper and distance and the shadows of cliff and cloud.

Toward the heart of this sanctuary wilderness come the rivers, the Green from the north, the Yampa from the east. Their color, which in all seasons except that of extreme low water is yellow-tawny with silt, betrays the inadequate soil-conservation, the over-grazing, the wastage of precious topsoil, upstream. Is it only in our minds that they suddenly seem purer as they sweep through the portals of both water trails into the Monument? Dropping lower over the canyons and the sunny openings of the parks and holes, you can see how they break into sparkling white-capped riffles, and flash back light poured on them from above, and darken under the overhanging shadows of cliffs, and how they finally come together under the great curving fin of Steamboat Rock, and together cut through the rock west and south to burst out of the millrace of Split Mountain Canyon into the semi-desert of the Uinta Valley.

Down here is the quarry of fossil dinosaur bones, well worth a visit and easy to see even if, like many visitors, you have only a few hours of time. At the Monument Headquarters nine miles from Jensen and Highway 40 you can explore the diggings from which paleontologists have taken 350 tons of fossils representing twelve different kinds of dinosaurs. You can see some (and shortly will be able to see more) silicified bones embedded in the quarry walls. In the museum nearby you will find recognizable bones and a dioramic history of the reptilian life of the late Jurassic period. The still-rather-skimpy scale of the display as of 1955, and the imperfectly developed setting, may remind you that here as elsewhere the Park Service must serve without sufficient funds to do the really first-rate job it is able and eager to do.

Perhaps, like most tourists, you have made this eighteen-mile detour in the belief that the little clay-and-rock bowl in which Headquarters is situated is all the Monument has to offer. There are not even pictures (there should be photomurals!) to indicate the variety and beauty that lie back in the canyons a few miles upstream. Even the name "Dinosaur" will delude you if you don't already know, or don't prospect for yourself. But the drive up from Jensen may have given you a hint of what one trip over by air would have impressively confirmed. For coming up from Jensen you faced the grand panorama of Split Mountain, notched darkly where the Green River emerges from it. That is the southern gate of Dinosaur's canyons. Drive three miles over and take a look.

Close up, it is not so impressive. You look at the lowest cliffs, and they hide the great gash that was seen from afar. So follow the riverside meadows south for a mile and look again. The perspective is right once more: the south half of Split Mountain, white and knobbed and gouged like a dinosaur spine, stands before you beyond the swift, silent river. With a rowboat or life raft, you can pull across to one of Dinosaur's special little paradises—nature-trail country if such there ever was.

In a draw made to order for pleasant walking, you parallel the outside face of Split Mountain, passing a succession of slots or narrow gorges through which you can see barely enough to know that there is something mysterious and exciting beyond. Take your choice of them and go on in.

You follow a stream course, now in it, now on a rock shelf above. After a time it will suddenly strike you: what happened to the desert? This surely doesn't belong—this sudden chill twilight, these firs and maples and birches and bowers of orchids and ferns. No rustle of cottonwoods or rasp of cicadas here—only the flute call of a hermit thrush and the tinkle of water under the sedges.

Some light shows through dark boughs up ahead. In a moment you emerge into a vast room, as high-walled as it is wide. Now the barrier is behind you and you're really on Split Mountain—not in the split itself, for that's where the noisy river is, but face to face with the naked castellated wall that hides it. If you are a climber, you'll be glad to find the rock firm and not slick. You will see that for all the depth of these massive formations, they run in layers, criss-crossed with ledges that will lead you to the top of the ridge high above the rushing Green. From this vantage point you can look into Dinosaur's Zion—more spiry than Zion but a true counterpart in color: chocolate and red, pink and purple and white and golden tan, its lower talus overgrown with sage and dotted with junipers, its heights dark with conifers. And here on top you can stride along the wind-swept plateau past towering columns and steeples, past gulf after gulf of the kind by which you climbed from the valley. It has been a long climb, but the mountains always save their greatest rewards for climbers.

THIS IS ONE WAY to taste Dinosaur if you have only a day for a quick loop up from Highway 40. But it is only a taste; though you have scanned the Green from Moonshine Draw to Red Wash, that has shown you only the last five miles of the 120 miles of superlative river country contained within the Monument. When you're coming down the river, Split Mountain is the climax that you approach with your heart pounding, but on the ground, even from the rim, it is only the teaser that traps your imagination. Some hours later you may find yourself turning off the blacktop of U.S. 40 opposite the Bonanza road, twelve miles east of Jensen, for a look at what's beyond the range.

The look may take you a day or a week. All the time you can spare won't be too much, for this country will show you canyons and riverside campgrounds of a kind not to be found elsewhere in our national parks. And even then, no road or combination of roads will show you more than a small part. You will know this Monument only when you have lived with it, on the river, going in boats.

Still, even the roads provide adventure. Once off the hardened mud flats, you climb onto one of the well-graded Moffat County (Colorado) roads that thread the summit of the great Blue Mountain plateau. You are heading away from all pavement, gas stations, inns, and stores. It will take a full tank of gas to get you into Echo Park and out again; if you plan any side exploring, take a jeep can or two.

The roads, though primitive, are well marked. If you can't contentedly adjust your pace to the roads, and if you hate the whine of low gear, both you and your car will be happier elsewhere. But if you will ease into the dips, crawl with care over the rocky pitches, and stay away from muck and loose sand, you'll get along very well.

Twelve miles from the highway, just as you break out onto the low-lying mountaintop, the road forks. The right fork goes east, past Youghall, to the old Mantle Ranch road, and on back to join the highway at Elk Springs. The left fork leads to the heart of the Monument. It seems to give the lie to all the warnings you've heard, as you breeze along at fifty miles per hour, and you wonder why you bothered with the shovel and extra jack. After six miles of it you might as well take the spur route to Round Top. If you needed an education in mountain roads, this will give you the postgraduate course. Three miles seem like thirty, and unless you have a jeep or pickup you'll never drive quite to the lookout, but you can reach a breath-taking perch on the rim a mile or so west of it.

Far below, beyond a belt of quaking aspen, is the whole broad sweep of carved-ivory Yampa canyons, from Harper's Corner east to Douglas Mountain, with even a bit of the river in view down in Castle Park. Walk over to the lookout and you can look down into Castle Park through a telescope. The glass puts you right on top of Charley Mantle's henhouse! Most of the ranch is hidden behind cliffs. The whole cut-up plateau spreads out below you—magnificent, sun-smitten, silent. On the horizon is the gray-brown pyramid of Zenobia Peak, with just a hint of Lodore's depths to its left.

Back on the county road, you can look forward to the rest of the trip with the reassurance that comes of knowing you've conquered the worst road of all—and you still haven't crossed the line into Dinosaur National Monument. You swing back into Utah, still on a road maintained by Moffat County, Colorado. This part is all fine going, over wide open highlands where you see deer and sage grouse and free-roaming horses. You're moving back in time, to where this pneumatic ride and Duco and chrome don't quite belong. There's a waterhole, a log cabin, a sheepherder's lonely sagging covered wagon and dogs. . . .

Before heading down the steep zigzags of Iron Springs Wash into Echo Park you'll want to look into the canyon maze from Harper's Corner, southwestern clog of the horseshoe of Echo Park. It's an easy drive on a spur road. A few rods out on the short trail from the parking-area, a few steps along the catwalk of that last narrowing, exposed ridge bring you to the flattened, slightly elevated final cape; your gaze sweeps over 360 degrees of unspoiled natural beauty for as far as you can see.

With your binoculars again, follow it clockwise from the direction of your approach: to the left the walls plunge from your feet into the swirling water of Whirlpool Canyon 2,400 feet below. The near wall is spectacularly ridged with knife-edges between tremendous scoop-outs close-set with Douglas firs. You can look down on the green delta of Jones Creek, and ten miles downstream, through a breach in the tilted mountains, you can see the emerald pastures of Island Park. To the right, just as precipitous, is the great amphitheater of Echo with the mile-long fin of Steamboat rising in the center. There is a peep into Lodore, and a glimpse of the Green swinging out, disappearing behind Steamboat, then emerging, swelled by the

Yampa, in its almost circumferential switchback. From Harper's Corner, too, you can look into the final sculptured canyons of the Yampa. Nearer yet, almost at your feet, are the green alfalfa fields, the meadows, the curving line of willow and box elder, which make up the floor of Echo Park.

Whether you count your remaining sunrises in hundreds or in thousands, you could still do no better than to camp for the night among the piñons here and wait to see the sun come up over Blue Mountain and flood down into these blue canyons.

On the way into Echo Park the road levels out after the Iron Springs grade to skirt the head of Pool Creek Canyon, here a breathtaking little gash sliced deep in sandstone. Farther on is Sand Canyon. You drive down the bottom of it, but it has been worked over so much by the Park Service that it holds few terrors now. When you come out of it, you can go left to Echo Park or right to Castle Park. Echo is the nearer and better known. The road ends right beside the junction of the Yampa and the Green.

What can you do here? Not very much, really. Only the healing things for which the national parks are kept inviolate. You may camp, walk, climb, look, listen to the calls of wild geese flying the canyon airways. You may test the perfect acoustics of Steamboat Rock and hear your words come back as clearly as you uttered them. Lie on a sandy bank and watch the myriad sunbursts flash and sparkle at you through the maple leaves. Swim—the whole Park is a beach. Hunt fossils in the formations that yield them. Visit Pat Lynch's retreat, or duck into the mysterious coolness of Whispering Cave. If you have a horse and the water is low enough, you can follow the Yampa four miles upstream through some of its best canyon, fording it a half-dozen times until you reach Warm Springs.

Back on the Yampa bench, a road goes east through good horseback country to Hell's Canyon and Mantle's Ranch. Studying the map, you will be surprised to learn that where you cross Red Rock Canyon you're actually outside the Monument, as you were at Iron Springs Wash, on upper Pool Creek, and in Sand Canyon. Something is certainly wrong with Dinosaur's section-line border here.

The road passes near some fine overlooks. At one point you can see into Castle Park's excavated Basketmaker cave. Then upper Hell's Canyon breaks dramatically out of the rim country on your right, just beyond Round Top. The road dips into a shallow place near its mouth and divides into two forks, both rough. The right-hand one follows the bench eastward past Harding Hole to climb over the far end of Blue Mountain at the head of Thanksgiving Gorge. The left fork follows the bed of deepening lower Hell's Canyon for a couple of miles to Castle Park.

The cattle-ranching Mantles are not always at home, but if you do find them at their frontier house in its cliff-ringed setting of orchards and gardens and pasture, your visit to Dinosaur will be immeasurably enriched. They are the living pioneers of the region, sensitive to its charms and bent on preserving them.

Castle Park is a good base for exploring. Camping is pleasant along the river downstream, or in Hell's Canyon with water available from the Mantles' spring. Mantle' s Cave is Dinosaur's best-known archæological site, but the area abounds in others that haven't been touched—and shouldn't be, except by an authorized scientific expedition. You can boat or swim across the river and follow a tricky series of ledges into a hanging valley where there are unexcavated ruins in the shelter of arching overhangs. Broken artifacts are scattered through the gullies there, and in a deep cave behind a usually dry waterfall there is a crudely furnished log shelter: either one of Pat Lynch's various dwellings or the lair of some old-time outlaw.

From your Castle Park camp, you can easily and safely take a one-day trip on the river, through a superb stretch of its canyon. The run starts upstream near Bull Park and ends at Mantle's Ranch. You will need a boat that is light enough to carry; a canoe, kayak, or small inflatable life raft will do. For making the trip in small boats, life jackets are always good insurance. It is about four miles by road to a point shown as elevation 5,854 on the topographic map of the Monument. Here you must leave the car and walk, carrying lunch and boat down a sandy ridge to the river. The river route back to the ranch is much longer than the road, but it can be covered in less than half a day when the water is reasonably fast. The perfect natural camp sites along the way, however, may tempt you to stretch the trip into two or three days. There are dramatic side canyons to explore; there are the mighty Grand Overhang and other sheer walls carved and polished by the river; there are white sand beaches to bask on, and caverns to pull into for the cool of their shade. Beaver come up alongside your boat and float with you. Deer stand and watch you pass. Swallows survey you from mud nests under rock eaves close overhead. Families of geese, momentarily caught in cross-currents, swim furiously to keep out of your reach, but seldom bother to fly.

From journey's end at Castle Park, it is not too long a hike back to where you left the car above Harding Hole. You can just as safely make the much longer run from Castle Park to Echo Park—the Yampa's rapids are upstream from Harding—but getting back to the car may be a difficulty. For parties traveling with two cars, the problem is solved.

AND EVEN A FEW HOURS on the river will convince you that what the "nature-lovers" have been saying is true. There is no place in our National Park System like Dinosaur. Every national park and monument preserves something theoretically unique and irreplaceable. What is unique about Dinosaur is its canyon rivers. Though other rivers of the West—in fact, almost all of them—have cut fantastic gorges and great canyons, they may only be admired and marveled at, seldom enjoyed. They remain aloof and impersonal. In Dinosaur you can live with the rivers and their canyons intimately and safely.

For boating in any part of the Monument except the lower Yampa, the right equipment and a good deal of know-how are essential. The streams are no more to be feared than water anywhere else, the biggest waves in them are no worse than a good rolling surf, the canyons are no more dangerous than mountains anywhere. Simply approach them with reasonable respect and you will find them friendly and exceedingly pleasant to know.

Sooner or later, having tasted the lotus, you will have to take the full river trip through Dinosaur. The easy route, taken each year by increasing hundreds of all ages, starts at Lily Park on the Yampa, winds forty-five miles through deepening canyons to Echo Park, and then goes on down the Green through Whirlpool Canyon and Island Park to the last climactic run through Split Mountain Canyon. Oddly enough, Dinosaur has been perfectly engineered for amateurs of all degrees of skill and daring, for the rough water begins as riffles—beginners' slopes—and progresses through minor rapids to the two big power mills of Split Mountain. You may take as much or as little of white water as you like, and walk around it all if you choose. Each day's experience fits you for what comes tomorrow. If you come out of the sluiceway of Split Mountain still unsatisfied by SOB and Moonshine, you have only to truck your boat to the Gates of Lodore and take on the real heavyweight. Before doing any of it, you will want to discuss your plans with the ranger at Headquarters, and you will probably take his advice and leave all the arrangements to Bus Hatch, of Vernal, who will furnish everything you need, including an accommodating boatman-guide, for less than it would cost you to go on your own.

At the Gates of Lodore, on the Green, you are lulled by deceptive calm, but on the Yampa your canyon entrance is marked by deceptively choppy water. You leave the Vale of Tears (that's its name) as you cross the Monument boundary. First camp is usually at Anderson Hole. From there you can push on to Bull Park in one day if you wish, but there are innumerable benches of cottonwood and box elder for camp sites. Clear spring water can be found in certain spots, but it is not essential; the river water is just as drinkable and has, as they say, more "body." Camp where you please, whenever you get tired or want to stay awhile.

It is in the stretch between Anderson Hole and Bull Park that the Yampa has its three rapids. They can be spotted on the map at Tepee Hole, Five Springs Draw, and Big Joe Draw. If you want, you can walk around all of them, but after studying them you will find them safe to navigate even in small boats. At high water they are splashy and fast—they will seem plenty big enough at this stage of your training— but you will look back on them as mere outsize riffles when you have experienced the roller-coaster ride of Split Mountain. Actually they are just right for foldboats, and have been run on inflated air mattresses.

The first stop on the Yampa that can be reached by road you already know: Castle Park. The next, after a day of drifting past the Tiger Wall and other magnificent cliffs, is Echo Park. Then you have a short day of swift water to Jones Hole, a midway point of Whirlpool Canyon, and one of the finest camp sites on the river. Here is clear water, a treat after several days of drinking the topsoil of Colorado and Wyoming. Here too are not the catfish and "Colorado River Salmon" that the Monument provides elsewhere, but trout—big, numerous, and hungry. And up the lovely side gorge of Jones Creek is one of the finest of all Dinosaur's walks.

Jones Hole is your last camp site. From there on, it is a short, exciting day's run. The rest of Whirlpool takes but an hour: there is real power in the river now, and an unremitting downhill plunge. Then you're out in the calm meanders of Island Park, where hospitable Joel Evans has his ranch.

Here, as in Castle Park and Echo Park, is a wide and sunny place to loiter for a day or two, riding, climbing, or just loafing. Blue Mountain, its grand anticline exposed to view, still hems you in on the left, but on the right there are only low bare foothills.

Through Island Park the river carries you into Rainbow Park, where the tortured uplift of red and chocolate stone, hacked through by the Green, tells you you are at the gates of the famous Split Mountain Canyon. You will want to rest here, swim, eat lunch, and reflect on the cataracts you have been told lie just ahead.

Split Mountain Canyon has two big booming rapids. The first is called Moonshine, the second, for obvious reasons, SOB. Below them are Schoolboy and one other. Schoolboy, according to Bus Hatch's son Don, "tries to be bad but isn't." Moonshine and SOB are not to be trifled with. Mismanaged, they can capsize the best boat that has ever been on the Green, and even the rubber rafts must be piloted with skill. Run smartly by an oarsman who knows his business, they provide a wonderfully exciting, spray-drenched ride full of inaudible shouting. A skillful foldboatman will find them navigable provided his boat has splash covers over the cockpit. And again the rivers have been considerate: you may walk around all of Split Mountain's rapids, lining your boat down on a rope. Indeed, you could probably walk the length of the canyon on either side without getting your feet wet.

All in all, Split Mountain is a fitting climax to your first river trip through Dinosaur National Monument. If you are really bitten by now, there is still Lodore.

The whole of this book could deal with Lodore and not tell its story. Much has been said about its soaring red walls, reddest where they catch the light of a setting sun, purple in the deep-cut shadows. Lodore looms big in the journals of Ashley, Powell, the Kolbs. Though infinitely shorter, it presents navigational problems as touchy as those of the Grand Canyon. And its scenery is of an altogether different order from that of the Yampa—different in size, in sculpture, and in coloring. The Yampa is of the desert, a long Canyon de Chelly blessed with the magic carpet of moving water. Lodore is of the mountains. Its pines, its rocks, its terraced cliffs sometimes half a mile high, its impatient river everywhere full of chop and swirl, all confirm the thought. In Lodore the Green cuts straight through Dinosaur's highest country, a region of ponderosa pine and stunted aspen, juniper and mountain mahogany, faint trails and dim wheel tracks mostly leading nowhere.

By land you can poke into the best of this high region from Greystone (pop. 2), reached from U.S. Highway 40, or Colorado 318. For all the lack of road-improvement, it is often surprising how well packed the clay is, how firm and smooth the sand, how nicely fitted the rocks into a negotiable flagstone pattern. Can it be that you are beginning to feel at home on the wild, wild trails?

Your car nearly makes the summit of Zenobia itself. Look at the view. It's vast, but oh, how vulnerable! You look far beyond the protection of the Monument boundaries, and you wonder what a few uranium-hunters

Steamboat Rock in Echo Park.

could do to this panorama. You see what grazing has already done here, and you ask if the Monument is big enough to save a representative buffer for its canyons.

The edge of Lodore is within easy walking distance. Go over and look down: you'll have to go through that slot—not this moment maybe, but as soon as you can get boat and boatman together and drive to the gates.

Elsewhere in the Monument you might debate whether you need a river guide. Here there is only one answer: you do. Here there is no substitute, even dumb luck, for experience and competence. Recognizing the landmarks, which vary greatly at different stages of water, is difficult, and if you don't recognize the landmarks you may drift into one of the big rapids under the impression that it is some minor riffle. It was this kind of groping in the dark that caused some of the early rivermen to take weeks getting through Lodore when in fact its entire length can be run in a day.

Lodore's churning river allows no rest. There is always a channel choked with great rocks, a bar, a snag, a suspicious hump in the water's pour. Tail waves, fanning down between obstructions, are sport for the pounding boats. You might as well get used to them and enjoy them, for you'll be crossing through them or riding their backs almost to the sudden stillness of Echo Park.

There are three rapids that are first-class by any standard. They are Upper Disaster Falls (at high water Lower Disaster is practically imaginary), Triplet Falls, and Hell's Half Mile. Upper Disaster is as dramatic as any of them. It makes a beautiful, exciting run, but unless you have a spare boat along to pick up the stragglers in the event of an upset, the discreet thing to do is to "cheat" it by sneaking along the left bank. Or by walking around.

Next is Triplet—a fast three-stage chute-the-chutes, as its name implies. Right at its foot is an excellent camp site—if one can favor a particular site in a canyon that is one long campground from end to end. If you have passed up the lure of the lovely pine-forested isles at the mouth of Pot Creek, however, you will surely settle down for the night on this shadowy Triplet beach.

Hell's Half Mile is yet to come. Above it the river is so still that you can plainly hear the wingbeats of a blue heron flying upstream. But watch out! The fall comes sudden and the waves so high that you can't see the jutting rocks beyond them. Like Lava Falls in the Grand Canyon, this mighty Hell's Half Mile is usually portaged.

The carry is easy along the right bank. After a hundred feet you are past the first shattering drop, and can launch out once more into the tailrace. Except for the innocent-looking Rippling Brook Rapid, which can sink you, you're through the rough water of Lodore. The Green is resting now, and so can you. Echo Park is coming up. You know what lies beyond.

SO YOU HAVE SEEN Dinosaur, lived with it. The place has made no special demand on your purse, your energies, or even on your car, if you took it easy. But it has made itself a special spot in your heart and your memory. The scenes you saw there will return again and again to your mind, and so will some of the people: Jess Lombard, the Monument superintendent, or Harry Robinson, the historian; Joel Evans and the Mantles; Bus Hatch, one

Yampa Canyon, Box Elder Park.

Whirlpool Canyon from Harpers Corner.

Yampa River, downstream from Castle Park.

Preparators on Quarry face.

Hells Canyon Ranch in Castle Park, Yampa Canyon.

of the authentic rivermen, who has tested his skill on hundreds of miles of white water, including the Grand Canyon.

And what of the canyon rivers of Dinosaur? Are they worth more as kilowatts? At least you know that no other national park or monument reserves for you and your children, unspoiled, anything like them. Outside there are other canyons—Glen, the San Juan, Cataract and Labyrinth, even the big Grand itself. But, for all their majesty, not one can give you what these Dinosaur canyons give: elbow room, space, sport, the sense of being an intimate part of the living world. If you are like other people, you may come to feel that you have never lived so deeply or so satisfyingly as you did during your brief journey into the rock paradise where the Green and Yampa meet.

The National Park Idea

Alfred A. Knopf

DINOSAUR NATIONAL MONUMENT, established in 1915 and enlarged in 1938, is a part of the National Park System, and to be a part of that system is to be dedicated to certain clearly defined principles and uses. A National Park or Monument is a scenic or archæological or in some way unique preserve, and it is also playground, campground, natural schoolroom, wildlife sanctuary. It is not a resort, though there will always be those who try to make it so. And the very special purposes of recreation, education, refreshment, and inspiration for which Parks and Monuments have been set aside prohibit many economic uses which are thoroughly legitimate elsewhere.

Dinosaur is actually a year older than the service which administers it, but it and all other Parks and Monuments are operated according to the organic law which created the National Park Service in 1916. That Act of Congress ordered the conservation of "the scenery and the national and historic objects and the wild life" of the designated regions, and provided for "the enjoyment of the same in such manner and by such means *as will leave them unimpaired for the enjoyment of future generations.*"

The key word is "unimpaired," and the dictionary defines it as "not to diminish in quantity, value, or strength; not to injure or weaken or make worse; not to harm, hurt, mar, or spoil." It is an important point to remember.

There persists an old confusion between the National Parks and the National Forests—two very different things. The Forests provide the people, all the people, with magnificent facilities for recreation, and with vital watershed protection, and so do the Parks. But there the similarity ends. For the Forests are consistently put to economic use under policies prescribed by Congress and administered by the National Forest Service, a bureau of the Department of Agriculture. The Forests sell lumber and grazing, and can be developed for mining, irrigation, and power. The Parks sell nothing, although, like the Forests, they contract with concessioners to supply food and lodging and services to visitors. The Forests are open to grazing, under permit, and as a result have their troubles with some cattlemen. The same cattlemen yearn for grazing permits in the Parks, but there, in principle at least, they do not get them. Where cattle are seen in what appear to be Park lands, these are lands still held in private ownership within the Park's borders, and the Service is making every effort to eliminate them. Or the stock-owners are holders of pre-park permits which will not be renewed after their lifetime.

The Parks are set aside for other than dollar uses, to be kept without impairment for the enjoyment of the people. They cannot tolerate exploitation of any resource, for exploitation uses up, makes over, mars, and changes the things that according to wise law must be kept natural. If a tree falls in a Park, unless it blocks a road or endangers a building or human life it must lie where it has fallen, slowly to return to the earth out of which it grew. Grass can renew itself if properly used and cared for; so can a forest. But a mountain or a canyon or archæological remains cannot. If you cut a great swath up a hillside to put in a ski lift, the gash will remain for a very long time, perhaps long after you have abandoned the lift. If you flood a canyon, as it is proposed to flood the Dinosaur canyons with dams in Echo Park and Split Mountain, that canyon is gone forever, buried first under water and eventually under silt. And the lake you create will not be there for many generations to see or use. It has been stated on good authority that 38 percent of our dams have a useful life of under fifty years. Four hundred thousand tons of sediment are dumped into Lake Mead, on the Colorado, every twenty-four hours. You do not ever dig canyons out from under that kind of load. And the Green and Yampa are silt-laden where they flow through the Dinosaur canyons.

Moreover, no permanent growth can take hold on the shores of a reservoir if the water fluctuates as much as ten feet. The margin of any draw-down reservoir is a broad ugly mudbank except at extreme high water—and the average reservoir is full no oftener than once in four years. When I saw it in October 1954, the lake behind Fontana Dam in the Great Smokies was something dismal to behold. After three dry summers the water had receded many, many yards, exposing bleak banks of dried mud, bare of vegetation of any sort. There is no pleasure in sailing on such a lake as that, no pleasure in swimming in it, certainly none in looking at it, and the fishing has been well described as "honeymoon fishing." Some idea of what would happen to the scenery in Dinosaur if the proposed Echo Park dam were to go in can be gained from reminding oneself that the lake impounded behind this dam would fluctuate in depth 208 feet between the thirty-to-forty-year wet and dry cycles. When full, the lake would be 107 miles long and would cover 43,000 acres. When periodically drawn down to its silt pool, it would be about 70 miles long and cover about 9,000 acres. That leaves 34,000 acres of pretty drearily impaired scenery at low water.

The National Parks embrace areas of great natural beauty, of a splendor on which man cannot hope to improve. Who that has seen Glacier, Yosemite, Yellowstone, or the Tetons can doubt this? Simply to travel through them with open eyes is an uplifting and ennobling experience. The figures on what the Service calls "visitation"—a horrible word—demonstrate that the people need and want and use the Parks. Indeed, as one writer remarked, the people are loving the Parks to death. City and suburban folk increasingly feel the need to get away into the quiet and beauty of unspoiled natural scenery, and for this sort of recreation—an ambiguous word at best—the Parks are supreme, though the Forests, especially some of the designated wilderness areas, may be a close second.

Forty-two million people visited the National Parks, Monuments, and Historical Sites in 1953. Cut that number in half to allow for those who visited more than one Park and for those who made pilgrimages to the Statue of Liberty and the Franklin D. Roosevelt home in Hyde Park. Allow further for those who go to a Park looking for what isn't there—golf, tennis, night clubs, and resort activities—and there remain probably between fifteen and twenty million separate users of the National Park areas. That number, moreover, increases by ten percent every year in spite of the inadequate budgets and strained facilities on which the Service is forced to operate. Think what the Parks give those millions of Americans: honest, intelligent information, exhibits, demonstrations, museums and lectures and films that explain the Park's geology, history, flora and fauna. As public education there is nothing to approach it. There is no charge, once the trifling entrance fee is paid: you take as much or as little as you want. You make use of the good trails provided for hikers and riders, the good campgrounds, the hotel and cottage and cabin accommodations at rates controlled by the government. You enjoy roads that are unmarred by signboards, that ease through forests and mountains and canyons with a minimum of scarring of the natural beauty, so that driving is not a tense duel with death along a strip of man-made ugliness but a restful and enriching experience.

In a Park a citizen gets back something, and in a form he sees and appreciates, for the taxes he pays. No one can watch Park rangers or archæologists or naturalists working with visitors without being impressed by the eagerness of the visitors to be informed and the pleasure they take in what is given them. And there is something about the atmosphere of a National Park that makes people behave well—much better, for instance, than many Americans traveling abroad. Perhaps this general decency of behavior arises from some consciousness of the friendliness and good order of the Parks, the air of cheerful public service on a completely impartial and democratic basis. Perhaps it springs from an awareness that the supreme experience of solitude, the blessing of almost absolute quiet, is only a short distance away from the crowds.

With so many friends, it is difficult to understand why the Parks are so bedeviled by threats, and seem always to be fighting for their very existence. The story is an old one. There are frequent occasions when people see nothing wrong with harming, hurting, marring, or spoiling when there are valuable resources of water, power, timber, oil, or minerals to be exploited within Park boundaries. The Service, moreover, is not always in a position to make a vigorous defense. For one thing, it is always short of money. It is small, as federal bureaus go, and the small bureau often has a hard time getting money from Congress. Thus Congress, the very branch of government which set them aside, sometimes offers a threat—of omission—to the Parks. Other threats are not so indirect.

Thirty-five years ago one George K. Davol wanted to build a cableway across the Grand Canyon of the Colorado. To Stephen T. Mather, the first Director of the National Park Service, this seemed, as it would seem to almost anyone today, simply monstrous. John Barton Payne, his Secretary of the Interior, supported Mather's denial of the request, and that was that. Another proposal called for the building of an elevator alongside the 308-foot Great Falls of the Yellowstone. And Secretary Franklin K. Lane was at one time eager to use Yellowstone Lake—the largest body of water in America at so great an altitude, 7,731 Feet—for irrigation. That would have made it a draw-down reservoir, with results to its beauty that we can imagine but do not like to visualize. In his 1919 report, Mather wrote: "Is there not some place in this great nation of ours where lakes can be preserved in their natural state; where we and all generations to follow us can enjoy the beauty and charm of mountain waters in the midst of primeval forests? The country is large enough to spare a few such lakes and beauty spots. The nation has wisely set apart a few national parks where a state of nature is to be preserved. If the lakes and forests of these parks cannot be spared from the hand of commercialization, what hope can there be for the preservation of any scenic features of the mountains in the interest of posterity?"

The story of the years-long attempt by Ralph Henry Cameron, onetime Senator from Arizona, to keep the Grand Canyon region from being adequately developed as a Park is too long to tell here. Mining-claims were the chief basis of Cameron's power, and only the Supreme Court was able finally to polish him off.

There are always some people who want to mine in the Parks, cut timber, graze cattle, build ski lifts and aerial tramways, turn into four-lane super-highways the roads that now are quiet and self-effacing and built so that those who drive them can see in peace and relaxation what they came to see. There is constant pressure to develop resort and recreational facilities which could not be placed in any Park without impairing it for the present as well as for future generations. Such facilities, moreover, are not needed in the Parks; they exist in abundance outside, in hundreds of resort areas as well as on most Reclamation lakes and to a limited degree within the National Forests.

Greatest of all threats to the Parks today is the pressure to build dams. The Bureau of Reclamation is a big bureau with an annual budget many times larger than the National Parks could ever hope for, and with the additional opportunity of financing new projects with funds accruing from the sale of power. The long-range appeal is twofold: water for irrigation and hydroelectric power for homes, farms, and industry. There is a local, short-range appeal too: a big payroll and the business that results in the nearest town during the construction period. In the case of the proposed dams in Dinosaur, the nearest town would be Vernal, Utah. As one would expect, some of the most relentless propaganda for the dams comes from there.

In his 1920 report Mather foresaw the sort of threat that is now made to Dinosaur. Once anything like a power project is authorized in any National Park, he wrote, "it will not only be illogical but impossible to keep irrigation dams and ditches, and even commercial lumbering, out of all our national parks. Then the next step will be to open these areas to hunting in season, as is the case with the national forests. Once a small dam is authorized for irrigation or other purposes, other dams will follow. Once a small lake is raised and a small amount of timber is destroyed . . . once start the national parks toward national forest status, and it will be logically impossible to stop short of all. One misstep is fatal."

Every reasonably informed person knows how important water is to the mountain states. Every reasonably informed person wants to see us get on with a wise development of the Upper Colorado River Basin. There is good reason to believe that the public opposition which the proposed Echo Park and Split Mountain dams aroused in 1954 would not have been aroused if the dam sites had lain outside the boundaries of the National Monument and the question of a damaging precedent of raids against the Parks had not been involved.

This is not the place for a detailed summary of arguments pro and con, or for a debate of the controversial problems such as evaporation loss at Echo Park as compared with evaporation loss at alternative sites. On that particular issue the anti-dam forces had definitely the better of the argument in 1954, and forced Reclamation to scale down its previously announced figures by a very large amount. It was for that reason, probably, among others, that the 83rd Congress allowed the dam recommendations to die without coming to a vote. But the Parks win battles only; the war goes on forever.

Those who would protect the Parks and Monuments must rest their case always on the organic law that created the National Park Service. Any attempt to change that law would certainly bring on an instant and nation-wide and wholly bipartisan explosion of protest. The danger is not that the law will be repealed or changed, but that it will be whittled away through special concessions and permits. It is necessary to bear in mind Stephen Mather's wise warnings when an advocate of whittling insists that he intends to create no precedents. With the best intentions in the world, he could not help creating a precedent. His successors in office might not agree with him about precedents, and they would have his own precedent to use against him.

The people, to whom the Parks belong, should be given the full facts on which to base a judgment, whenever the question of intrusion on Park lands arises. The people, as taxpayers who foot the bill, should also know, with fair exactness, and from a responsible reviewing body, how much a reclamation project is going to cost them, whether in a Park or not. The Upper Colorado River Basin development will involve expenditures to give anyone pause.

The attitude of Americans toward nature has been changing—slowly, perhaps, but inexorably. Fifty thousand persons camped out in one Park, the Great Smokies, in a single summer month of 1954. That same summer I spent a night at Manitou Experimental Forest, in which a near-by campground, run by the Forest Service and at that moment without a water supply, was expected to be used by fifty thousand people before winter. In 1951 Glacier National Park had a half-million visitors; in 1953 it had more than 630,000. In that same year, the last for which total figures are available, Grand Canyon had 830,000 odd, Yellowstone 1,300,000, and Yosemite just short of a million. Those figures are impressive no matter how you take them. They mean that what the Parks and Monuments provide and preserve *without impairment* is increasingly appreciated and increasingly needed by more and more millions of American families.

In 1925 Mather said: "I believe that today the National Park Service is a model bureau from the standpoint of efficiency in expenditure of public monies, adherence to the federal budget system, individual output of employees, co-operation with other government bureaus, low overhead expenses, and high morale and public spirit of personnel." He could, if he were alive today, put it even more strongly. It is hard to imagine more dedicated people than those who run the Parks. I have never met a single one whom I would not be glad to meet again, and I have invariably regretted the time to say good-by. The range of their interests, their high intelligence, their devotion, make them a separate and wonderful breed. Their love of their work often takes the form—sometimes very strange!—of believing the place they are stationed at to be the best in the entire system. Most remarkable of all, perhaps, is their cheerful willingness to work hours far beyond what the law prescribes, and their pride in the job they and their associates are doing.

There remain a few personal words to be said about Dinosaur. It *is* hard to get to. The roads into the interior of the Monument are abominable, and they stretch for miles and miles. To get the best view of Steamboat Rock, where the Green and Yampa meet, you must make a long rough drive and then walk an up-and-down trail for three miles—either that, or you must come in by river.

But remember that Yellowstone, which in 1955 will have close to a million and a half visitors, was once even more inaccessible. And inaccessible though Dinosaur yet is, nearly a thousand people made a several-day river trip through it in 1954. Dinosaur is not expendable wasteland, not a profitless desert, but a scenic resource of incalculable value that has been preserved this long precisely because of its inaccessibility. As a wilderness playground, there is nothing wrong with it that appropriations and wise use couldn't quickly cure—that and one or two improved (and most carefully planned) roads. Then people by the tens of thousands could annually drive into it and float down its marvelous rivers, and their coming and going would leave the canyons virtually unmarked. It is from the rivers that Dinosaur can best be seen, for it is from the rivers that you see the full glory of the canyon colors. You cannot judge the Dinosaur country from black-and-white photographs, beautiful as those often are. They often make it look harsh, even forbidding. It isn't. It is colorful and warm, and the spectacular Canyon of Lodore must be seen to be believed.

Three days in Dinosaur in the summer of 1954, two of them in a boat running down the Green, convinced me that America has here scenery to rank with that of the very greatest of our Parks—and that is saying a great deal. It is scenery that could not survive dams at Echo Park and Split Mountain.

Dinosaur deserves to be more visited. If it were, there is no doubt that the American people, who can recognize a superlative thing when they see it, would once again, as in the past, line up in favor of the organic law of the National Parks Service and the dedicated and devoted men who run it. That is all it would take, that democratic groundswell, to insure that Dinosaur and the other superlative places will be passed on, unimpaired, to our grandchildren's grandchildren.